# BARRON'S BOOK NOTES

# WILLIAM SHAKESPEARE'S
# *Hamlet*

BY

**Michael Feingold**
Theater Critic
*The Village Voice*
New York City

SERIES EDITOR

**Michael Spring**
Editor, *Literary Cavalcade*
Scholastic Inc.

**BARRON'S**

BARRON'S EDUCATIONAL SERIES, INC.

## ACKNOWLEDGMENTS

We would like to thank Loreto Todd, Senior Lecturer in English, University of Leeds, England, for preparing the chapter on Elizabethan English in this book.

We would like to acknowledge the many painstaking hours of work Holly Hughes and Thomas F. Hirsch have devoted to making the *Book Notes* series a success.

*All inquiries should be addressed to:*
Barron's Educational Series, Inc.
250 Wireless Boulevard
Hauppauge, New York 11788

*Library of Congress Catalog Card No. 84-18448*

International Standard Book No. 0-8120-3417-1

**Library of Congress Cataloging in Publication Data**

Feingold, Michael.
  William Shakespeare's Hamlet.

  (Barron's book notes)
  Bibliography: p. 121
  Summary: A guide to reading "Hamlet" with a critical
and appreciative mind. Includes background on the author's
life and times, sample tests, term paper suggestions, and
a reading list.
    1. Shakespeare, William, 1564–1616. Hamlet.
[1. Shakespeare, William, 1564–1616. Hamlet. 2. English
literature—History and criticism] I. Title.
PR2807.F38   1984      822.3'3      84-18448
ISBN 0-8120-3417-1 (pbk.)

PRINTED IN THE UNITED STATES OF AMERICA

5 6 7 8    550    12 11 10

# CONTENTS

# HOW TO USE THIS BOOK

You have to know how to approach literature in order to get the most out of it. This *Barron's Book Notes* volume follows a plan based on methods used by some of the best students to read a work of literature.

Begin with the guide's section on the author's life and times. As you read, try to form a clear picture of the author's personality, circumstances, and motives for writing the work. This background usually will make it easier for you to hear the author's tone of voice, and follow where the author is heading.

Then go over the rest of the introductory material—such sections as those on the plot, characters, setting, themes, and style of the work. Underline, or write down in your notebook, particular things to watch for, such as contrasts between characters and repeated literary devices. At this point, you may want to develop a system of symbols to use in marking your text as you read. (Of course, you should only mark up a book you own, not one that belongs to another person or a school.) Perhaps you will want to use a different letter for each character's name, a different number for each major theme of the book, a different color for each important symbol or literary device. Be prepared to mark up the pages of your book as you read. Put your marks in the margins so you can find them again easily.

Now comes the moment you've been waiting for—the time to start reading the work of literature. You may want to put aside your *Barron's Book Notes* volume until you've read the work all the way through. Or you may want to alternate, reading the *Book Notes* analysis of each section as soon as you have finished reading the corresponding part of the original. Before you move on, reread crucial passages you don't fully understand. (Don't take this guide's analysis for granted—make up your own mind as to what the work means.)

Once you've finished the whole work of literature, you may want to review it right away, so you can firm up your ideas about what it means. You may want to leaf through the book concentrating on passages you marked in reference to one character or one theme. This is also a good time to reread the *Book Notes* introductory material, which pulls together insights on specific topics.

When it comes time to prepare for a test or to write a paper, you'll already have formed ideas about the work. You'll be able to go back through it, refreshing your memory as to the author's exact words and perspective, so that you can support your opinions with evidence drawn straight from the work. Patterns will emerge, and ideas will fall into place; your essay question or term paper will almost write itself. Give yourself a dry run with one of the sample tests in the guide. These tests present both multiple-choice and essay questions. An accompanying section gives answers to the multiple-choice questions as well as suggestions for writing the essays. If you have to select a term paper topic, you may choose one from the list of suggestions in this book. This guide also provides you with a reading list, to help you when you start research for a term paper, and a selection of provocative comments by critics, to spark your thinking before you write.

# THE AUTHOR AND HIS TIMES

William Shakespeare lived in a time of great change and excitement in England—a time of geographical discovery, international trade, learning, and creativity. It was also a time of international tension and internal uprisings that came close to civil war.

Under Elizabeth I (reigned 1558–1603) and James I (reigned 1603–1625), London was a center of government, learning, and trade, and Shakespeare's audience came from all three worlds. His plays had to please royalty and powerful nobles, educated lawyers and scholars, as well as merchants, workers, and apprentices, many of whom couldn't read or write. To keep so many different kinds of people entertained, he had to write into his plays such elements as clowns who made terrible puns and wisecracks; ghosts and witches; places for the actors to dance and to sing the hit songs of the time; fencing matches and other kinds of fight scenes; and emotional speeches for his star actor, Richard Burbage. There is very little indication that he was troubled in any way by having to do this. The stories he told were familiar ones, from popular storybooks or from English and Roman history. Sometimes they were adapted, as *Hamlet* was, from earlier plays that had begun to seem old-fashioned. Part of Shakespeare's success came from the fact that he had a knack for making these old tales come to life.

When you read *Hamlet*, or any other Shakespearean play, the first thing to remember is that the words are poetry. Shakespeare's audience had no movies, tele-

vision, radio, or recorded music. What brought entertainment into their lives was live music, and they
liked to hear words treated as a kind of music. They
enjoyed plays with quick, lively dialogue and jingling
wordplay, with strongly rhythmic lines and neatly
rhymed couplets, which made it easier for them to
remember favorite scenes. These musical effects also
made learning lines easier for the actors, who had to
keep a large number of roles straight in their minds.
The actors might be called on at very short notice to
play some old favorite for a special occasion at court,
or at a nobleman's house, just as the troupe of actors
in *Hamlet* is asked to play *The Murder of Gonzago*.

The next thing to remember is that Shakespeare
wrote for a theater that did not pretend to give its
audience an illusion of reality, like the theater we are
used to today. When a housewife in a modern play
turns on the tap of a sink, we expect to see real water
come out of a real faucet in something that looks like a
real kitchen sink. But in Shakespeare's time no one
bothered to build onstage anything as elaborate as a
realistic kitchen sink. The scene of the action had to
keep changing to hold the audience's interest, and to
avoid moving large amounts of scenery, a few objects
would be used to help the audience visualize the
scene. For a scene set in a kitchen, Shakespeare's company might simply have the cook come out mixing
something in a bowl. A housewife in an Elizabethan
play would not even have been a woman, since it was
considered immoral for women to appear onstage.
An older woman, like Hamlet's mother Gertrude,
would be played by a male character actor who spe-
cialized in matronly roles, and a young woman like
Hamlet's girlfriend Ophelia would be played by a
teenage boy who was an apprentice with the company. When his voice changed, he would be given adult

male roles. Of course, the apprentices played not only women, but also pages, servants, messengers, and the like. It was usual for everyone in the company, except the three or four leading actors, to "double," or play more than one role in a play. Shakespeare's audience accepted these conventions of the theater as parts of a game. They expected the words of the play to supply all the missing details. Part of the fun of Shakespeare is the way his plays guide us to imagine for ourselves the time and place of each scene, the way the characters behave, the parts of the story we hear about but don't see. The limitations of the Elizabethan stage were significant, and a striking aspect of Shakespeare's genius is the way he rose above them.

Theaters during the Elizabethan time were open-air structures, with semicircular "pits," or "yards," to accommodate most of the audience. The pit could also serve as the setting for cock fights and bear baiting, two popular arena sports of the time.

The audience in the pit stood on three sides of the stage. Nobles, well-to-do commoners, and other more "respectable" theatergoers sat in the three tiers of galleries that rimmed the pit. During breaks in the stage action—and sometimes while the performance was underway—peddlers sold fruit or other snacks, wandering through the audience and calling out advertisements for their wares.

The stage itself differed considerably from the modern stage. The main part, sometimes called the "apron" stage, was a raised platform that jutted into the audience. There was no curtain, and the audience would assume when one group of actors exited and another group entered there had been a change of scene. Because there was no curtain someone always carried a dead character off. It would, after all, have spoiled the effect if a character who had just died in the play got up in full view of the audience and walked off stage to make way for the next scene. The stage often had one or more trapdoors, which could be used for entry from below or in graveyard scenes.

Behind the main stage was a small inner stage with a curtain in front of it. During productions of *Hamlet*, the curtain served as the tapestry (or arras) that Claudius and Polonius hide behind when they spy on Hamlet, and later it was opened to disclose Gertrude's bedchamber.

Above the apron stage, on the second story, was a small stage with a balcony. In *Hamlet* this small stage served as a battlement and in *Romeo and Juliet* as the balcony in the famous love scene.

Still higher was the musicians' balcony and a turret for sound effects—drum rolls, trumpet calls, or thunder (made by rolling a cannon ball across the floor).

Now that you know something about the theater he wrote for, who was Shakespeare, the man?

Unfortunately, we know very little about him. A writer in Shakespeare's time was not considered special, and no one took pains to document Shakespeare's career the way a writer's life would be recorded and studied in our century. Here are the few facts we have.

Shakespeare was born in 1564, in the little English country town of Stratford, on the Avon River. He was the grandson of a tenant farmer and the son of a shopkeeper who made and sold gloves and other leather goods. We know that Shakespeare's family was well off during the boy's childhood—his father was at one point elected bailiff of Stratford, an office something like mayor—and that he was the eldest of six children. As the son of one of the wealthier citizens, he probably had a good basic education in the town's grammar school, but we have no facts to prove this. We also have no information on how he spent his early years or on when and how he got involved with the London theater.

At 18 he married a local girl, Anne Hathaway, who gave birth to their first child—a daughter, Susanna—six months later. This does not mean, as some scholars believe, that Shakespeare was forced into marriage: Elizabethan morals were in some ways as relaxed as our own, and it was legally acceptable for an engaged couple to sleep together. Two years later, Anne gave birth to twins, Hamnet (notice the similarity to "Hamlet") and Judith, but by this time Shakespeare's parents were no longer so well off. The prosperity of country towns like Stratford was declining as the city of London and its international markets grew, and so Shakespeare left home to find a way of earning a living. One unverified story says Shakespeare was driven out of Stratford for poaching (hunting without a license) on the estate of a local aristocrat; another says he worked in his early twenties as a country schoolmaster or as a private tutor in the home of a wealthy family.

Shakespeare must somehow have learned about the theater, because the next time we hear of him, at age 28, he is being ridiculed in a pamphlet by Robert Greene, a playwright and writer of comic prose. Greene called Shakespeare an uneducated actor who had the gall to think he could write better plays than a university graduate. One indication of Shakespeare's early popularity is that Greene's remarks drew complaints, and his editor publicly apologized to Shakespeare in Greene's next pamphlet. Clearly, by 1592 the young man from Stratford was well thought of in London as an actor and a new playwright of dignity and promise.

Though England at the time was enjoying a period of domestic peace, the danger of renewed civil strife was never far away. From abroad came threats from hostile Roman Catholic countries like Spain and France. At home, both Elizabeth's court and Shakespeare's theater company were targets of abuse from the growing English fundamentalist movement we call Puritanism. In this period, England was enjoying a great expansion of international trade, and London's growing merchant class was largely made up of Puritans, who regarded the theater as sinful and were forever pressing either the Queen or the Lord Mayor to close it down. Then there were members of Elizabeth's own court who believed she was not aggressive enough in her defiance of Puritans at home or Catholics abroad. One such man was the Earl of Essex, one of Elizabeth's court favorites (and possibly her lover), who in 1600 attempted to storm the palace and overthrow her. This incident must have left a great impression on Shakespeare and his company, for they came very close to being executed with Essex and his conspirators, one of whom had paid them a large sum to revive Shakespeare's *Richard II*, in which a weak king is forced to abdicate, as part of a propaganda campaign to justify Essex's attempted coup d'etat.

The performance, like the coup, apparently attracted little support. Elizabeth knew the publicity value of mercy, however, and Shakespeare's company performed for her at the palace the night before the conspirators were hanged. It can hardly be a coincidence that within the next two years Shakespeare wrote *Hamlet*, in which a play is performed in an unsuccessful attempt to depose a reigning king. The Essex incident must have taught him by direct experience the risks inherent in trifling with the power of the established political order.

Elizabeth's gift for keeping the conflicting elements around her in balance continued until her death in 1603, and her successor, James I, a Scots, managed to oversee two further decades of peace. James enjoyed theatrical entertainment, and under his reign, Shakespeare and his colleagues rose to unprecedented prosperity. In 1604 they were officially declared the King's Men, which gave them the status of servants to the royal household.

Shakespeare's son Hamnet died in 1596, about four years before the first performance of *Hamlet*. Whether he inspired the character of Hamlet in any way, we probably will never know. Some scholars have suggested that the approaching death of Shakespeare's father (he died in 1601) was another emotional shock that contributed to the writing of *Hamlet*, the hero of which is driven by the thought of his father's sufferings after death. This is only speculation, of course. What we do know is that Shakespeare retired from the theater in 1611 and went to live in Stratford, where he had bought the second biggest house in town, called New Place. He died there in 1616; his wife Anne died in 1623. Both Shakespeare's daughters had married by the time of his death. Because Judith's two sons both died young and Susanna's daughter Elizabeth—though she married twice and even became a baroness—had no children, there are no descendants of Shakespeare among us today.

On Shakespeare's tombstone in Stratford is inscribed a famous rhyme, putting a curse on anyone who dares to disturb his grave:

> Good friend, for Jesus' sake forbear
> To dig the dust enclosed here.
> Blest be the man that spares these stones,
> And curst be he that moves my bones.

The inscription had led to speculation that manuscripts of unpublished works were buried with Shakespeare or that the grave may in fact be empty because the writing attributed to him was produced by other hands. (A few scholars have argued that contemporaries like Francis Bacon wrote plays attributed to Shakespeare, but this notion is generally discredited.) The rhyme is a final mystery, reminding us that Shakespeare is lost to us. Only by his work may we know him.

# THE PLAY

## The Plot

Hamlet, prince of Denmark, is at school in Wittenberg, Germany, when his father, King Hamlet, dies. He comes home to Elsinore Castle to find his mother, Queen Gertrude, married to his uncle Claudius, the late king's younger brother. Claudius has had himself crowned king. Soldiers guarding Elsinore report to Hamlet through his friend Horatio that his father's ghost has been seen on the battlements. Hamlet goes with them to see the ghost, which speaks to him, saying that Claudius has murdered the king by pouring poison in his ear and that he, Hamlet, must avenge his father's murder. Hamlet swears to do this, but his philosophic mind is deeply upset at the shock of his uncle's treachery and his mother's possible involvement in it.

In the meantime, three related series of events are happening at the Danish court. First, the nations of Denmark and Norway have been engaged in border disputes with each other and with the neighboring country of Poland; King Hamlet became a hero in the eyes of his people by winning one such battle. Now Fortinbras, son of the late king of Norway, and nephew of the present, ailing king, wants Claudius' permission to march his army through Danish territory on the way to fight the Poles.

Second, Claudius' chief adviser, the elderly Polonius, is troubled by the behavior of his hot-headed son, Laertes, and his sensitive daughter, Ophelia. He is sending Laertes off to Paris to acquire polish and courtly manners, and instructs young Reynaldo to spy on him and report back if he falls into bad company. As for Ophelia, both Polonius and Laertes are concerned that she may be becoming too attached to young Hamlet, who has been sending her trinkets and love poems. They caution her to be careful, since it's not likely that the heir to the throne would marry someone below his royal station.

Third, Claudius and Gertrude are concerned over Hamlet's behavior, which was moody before the ghost spoke to him and has become increasingly disturbed, though they of course do not know why. They send for two of his school friends from Wittenberg, the Danish nobles Rosencrantz and Guildenstern, to try to discover the source of his moodiness. Arriving at the court, these two try to cheer Hamlet with news of a traveling company of actors on their way to Elsinore. This gives him a solution to one of his major worries—how to determine whether the ghost is really his father's spirit and is telling the truth, or is an evil spirit sent to tempt him into sin. He will have the actors put on a play about a courtier who poisons a king and seduces the queen. Claudius' reaction to the play will reveal the truth.

Meanwhile, Ophelia tells her father about a disturbing encounter she has had with Hamlet, who was behaving strangely. Polonius concludes that Hamlet's frustrated love for her has made him go mad. To prove this to Claudius, he has his daughter confront Hamlet in a corridor where he and the king can spy on them. Hamlet comes in, musing on death and whether or not he has the right to take a man's life. When Ophelia interrupts him, he becomes emotionally violent, denies he ever loved her, and urges her to go into a convent. Claudius is greatly upset by the scene, which makes him begin to fear that Hamlet has found out the truth about his father's death.

The performance of the play confirms Claudius' worst fears. During the pantomime prologue, Hamlet starts making double-edged remarks that drive Claudius out, angry and ashamed, when the actors have barely begun to speak. The court scatters in confusion, and Hamlet tells Horatio he is now totally convinced the ghost was telling the truth. Gertrude, furious with her son sends Rosencrantz and Guildenstern to tell him she wants to see him in private, in her chambers. On the way there Hamlet sees Claudius, defenseless, kneeling and attempting to pray. Hamlet thinks about killing him then and there, but holds back, believing that a man killed while praying would go to heaven, hardly a suitable punishment for Claudius' crimes. Hamlet cannot of course hear Claudius' thoughts, which are preoccupied with his inability to pray and his unwillingness to show true repentance by renouncing both the throne and his marriage to Gertrude.

Arriving at his mother's room, Hamlet is harsh and bitter with her, despite having promised himself (and earlier the ghost) to treat her gently. He accuses her of murder and incest—her new husband is her brother-in-law—attacking her so forcefully that Polonius, who has hidden behind a tapestry ("arras") in case she needs assistance, cries for help. Hamlet stabs what he thinks is Claudius, and is disappointed to learn he has killed only the meddling old man. Over the corpse, he tries to convince the now-frantic Gertrude to give up her second marriage. He is interrupted by the ghost, who reminds him that he has sworn to kill Claudius and leave his mother in peace. Their conversation convinces Gertrude, who cannot see the ghost, that her son is indeed mad.

In the meantime, Claudius has worked out a plan: He will send Hamlet, guarded by his former friends Rosencrantz and Guildenstern, on a diplomatic mission to England, carrying a sealed letter that asks the English king to arrest the troublesome heir and put him to death. After a bitter confrontation Rosencrantz and Guildenstern capture Hamlet and bundle him off to the ship bound for England. On the way there they pass Fortinbras' army marching to Poland. The sight makes Hamlet reflect on his failure to avenge his father, while Fortinbras is bringing honor to his.

When Ophelia learns of her father's death, she goes insane. Laertes returns from Paris, swearing vengeance on his father's murderer. The sight of his mad sister deflates his anger, and he allows Claudius to convince him that her madness is all Hamlet's fault. Meantime, Horatio learns that an unexpected stroke of luck has saved Hamlet's life: The ship he sailed on was attacked by pirates, who took him prisoner but let the others continue. Since Hamlet had discovered the treachery in Claudius' letter and replaced it with one requesting instead the execution of Rosencrantz and Guildenstern, the two have sailed to certain death. In return for the promise of ransom Hamlet is released by the pirates on the Danish coast.

Claudius, told of Hamlet's return, persuades Laertes to take his revenge in a formal duel, in which he will wound Hamlet with a poisoned sword. Before it takes place, the two have an unexpected clash in the graveyard where Ophelia, who has drowned herself, is being buried. Hamlet, who did not know of her death, is shocked into anger at the sight of Laertes leaping emotionally into the grave, and the two young men nearly get into a brawl over her coffin.

Having received Laertes' formal challenge, Hamlet apologizes to him graciously before the assembled court and the duel begins. They are evenly matched, so Claudius attempts to improve the odds by offering Hamlet a cup of poisoned wine, which, however, Queen Gertrude drinks. Laertes manages to wound Hamlet with the poisoned sword, but in the scuffle that follows they switch weapons and Laertes is wounded with it, too. Feeling the effect of the poisoned wine, Gertrude collapses, and the court finally realizes what Claudius has been up to. Hamlet at last achieves his revenge by stabbing Claudius with the poisoned weapon. Laertes, dying, confesses and begs Hamlet's forgiveness. Hamlet has just enough strength left to stop Horatio from drinking the dregs of the poisoned wine, and dies in his friend's arms, begging him to tell the world the true story. Fortinbras, whom Hamlet names as his successor, arrives in time to claim the throne and lament the horrible events.

# The Characters

## HAMLET

Hamlet may be the most complex character any playwright has ever placed onstage. Over the centuries critics have offered a multitude of explanations for Hamlet's behavior, but none of them has wholly been able to "pluck out the heart of my mystery," as Hamlet himself puts it. Eighteenth- and nineteenth-century theatergoers saw him as the classic ideal of the Renaissance courtier, poet, and philosopher. You can make a case for this view, since Hamlet often sees immediate events in a larger perspective. Ophelia's "O what a noble mind" speech is one of many suggesting that Shakespeare meant us to think of him this way.

Yet Hamlet is a deeply troubled young man who may strive for philosophy and poetry, but has in fact, by the end of the play, caused a good many violent deaths. While the earliest view was that Hamlet is simply a victim of circumstances, later critics saw him as a beautiful but ineffectual soul who lacked the strength of will to avenge his father. Passages in the play provide justification for this point of view, most notably in Hamlet's own soliloquies. Detractors of this view point out the cruel and barbaric aspects of Hamlet's behavior—his badgering of Ophelia, his rough treatment of Polonius' corpse, his reason for refusing to kill Claudius at prayer, and most of all the callous and seemingly unjust way he has Rosencrantz and Guildenstern put to death. To these commentators, either Shakespeare had badly assimilated such crudities from his source material, or Hamlet is himself a crude and unpleasant character, and his poetic speeches merely sugarcoat the bitter pill.

As the study of psychology developed into a science in the late nineteenth century, critics began applying its precepts to the play, viewing Hamlet as something close to a manic-depressive whose melancholy moods—as his failure to take revenge continues—deepened into self-contempt. This attitude draws some historical support from the Elizabethan belief that every human is dominated by one of four mental conditions called humors, each caused by the dominance in the body of one internal organ and its secretions. Hamlet, the notion runs, would have been seen by Shakespeare's contemporaries as a victim of the melancholy humor, which was especially associated with thinkers and philosophers. The trouble with this interpretation is that it does not explain Hamlet's frequent jokes and his many attempts at action.

The advent of Freudian psychology provided an additional twist to the "melancholy" interpretation. Freud's disciple Ernest Jones asserted that Hamlet was a victim of what Freudians call the Oedipus complex, that is, a desire to take his father's place in his mother's affections, a desire that would naturally trigger intense feelings of guilt if the father suddenly died. Jones' version, which partially inspired Sir Laurence Olivier's film adaptation (1948), is made believable by the intense overemphasis Hamlet puts on his mother's actions, despite the ghost's commands.

Many, many other explanations of Hamlet's motives have been offered, ranging from an excessive ambition that uses the ghost as a chance to seize the crown and then feels guilty about doing so, to an apathy that makes him hold back on philosophic grounds, since all action is futile. A few commentators have even proposed the unlikely possibility that Ham-

let is a woman who has been raised as a man to provide the throne with an heir, thus explaining Hamlet's
reluctance to commit the "masculine" act of
revenge.

What commentators and interpreters sometimes
forget is that Hamlet is first a character in a play, and
only secondly (if at all) a demonstration of this or that
view of human life. You might say that Hamlet is not
a classifiable *type of person* because he is *a specific person*,
who, like ourselves, is made up of many different
impulses and moods. It's possible for a soft-spoken
professor of philosophy, under the right circumstances, to commit murder, just as it's possible to be
depressed one day and crack jokes the next. Hamlet is
a person of exceptional intelligence and sensitivity,
raised to occupy a high station in life and then suddenly confronted with a violent and terrifying situation in which he must take drastic action. It's hardly
surprising to find him veering between extremes of
behavior, hesitating, demanding proof, looking for
the most appropriate way to carry out his task.

The fact that Hamlet is a thinking as well as a feeling
person, conscious of the good and bad points in every
step he takes, makes the act of revenge particularly
painful for him. Revenge is not Christian, and Hamlet
is a Christian prince; it is not rational, and Hamlet is a
philosopher; it is not gentle, and Hamlet is a gentleman.

Unlike the typical hero of an Elizabethan revenge
play (or a modern gangster movie), Hamlet does not
approach his task in an unquestioning, mechanical
way. He has qualms about it, as any of us might if
asked to do the same thing. It releases violent emotions in him, the intensity of which shocks and unbalances him. This questioning of what is instinctive and
preordained, the testing of the old tribal code by a

modern, troubled consciousness, is perhaps what makes the play so great and so universal in its interest.

As you read Shakespeare's play you will discover for yourself the specific things Hamlet says and does that make his motives understandable to you, just as every critic, reader, and playgoer over the centuries has picked the elements he or she most responded to in the young prince's tragic story. That will be *your* interpretation of *Hamlet*. If you follow the play closely and seriously, your opinions are likely to be every bit as valid as those of professional critics or teachers.

## OTHER CHARACTERS

Hamlet is the unquestioned center of the play. If he is not onstage he is almost always the subject of discussion in virtually every scene. Nevertheless, Shakespeare has taken pains to give the other characters as strong and independent an existence as possible. They are not mere foils for Hamlet, but distinct individuals who coexist and conflict with him, though their stories are told in a more fragmentary fashion.

### Gertrude

Hamlet's mother, the queen of Denmark, is a touching and mysterious figure. You never learn explicitly how much Gertrude knows about her husband King Hamlet's death, or how deeply she is attached to her new husband, Claudius. She never expresses her feelings, either, about the morality of marrying her brother-in-law, though this was considered incestuous at the time. But she expresses her concern for her son and her affection for Ophelia, plus (in the Closet Scene) a vague sense of guilt that only adds to the mystery about her. The ambiguity of Gertrude's position reaches its height in the final scene, when she drinks from the poisoned cup. Whether she knows it's poisoned is something you will have to decide for yourself.

## Claudius

The king of Denmark, Hamlet's uncle and later his stepfather, is shaped from a stock type familiar to Elizabethan theatergoers—the neglected younger brother who seeks to take over his older brother's title by unscrupulous means. Claudius, however, is a complex figure about whom Shakespeare gives you a good deal of information. You learn how the public attitude toward him has changed in Denmark (and changes again after Polonius' death); you learn about his drinking habits and his personal appearance as compared with his late brother's. Above all, you see him in action politically—manipulating, placating, and making pronouncements—and you see how his tactics in dealing with Norway or Poland link up to the conduct of his personal affairs. There is no question about his political ability, which is tied in with his talent for manipulating people and converting them to his point of view, as he does with Rosencrantz and Guildenstern. Some interpretations of the play suggest that we are meant to see him as more suited to the role of king than Hamlet is. His constant hypocritical smiling makes him easy to dislike, yet his genuine remorse in the Prayer Scene makes him more sympathetic, and hence more difficult for Hamlet to kill. Note that nowhere in the play does he directly express his feelings for Gertrude.

## The Ghost

Barnardo's remarks in the first scene make clear that the ghost is identical in appearance to the late King Hamlet. Hamlet's worry over whether it is "an honest ghost" is unusual for the time, an aspect of his intellectually probing nature. Ghosts were common figures in Elizabethan plays—an inventory of costumes for one theater included a cloak "for to go invisible." Belief in ghosts and omens was prevalent in England, and in the theater it was assumed that they could be trusted. Another long-standing but unverifiable tradition, incidentally, says the role of the ghost was played by Shakespeare himself, and was his greatest performance.

## Polonius

The father of Laertes and Ophelia is clearly a knowledgeable man. He holds an influential position at court, though the text never specifies what title he holds—or whether he is a holdover from King Hamlet's reign or newly appointed by Claudius, who appears to hold him in very high esteem. We know from Gertrude's reaction to his death that she is fond of him ("the good old man"), and that she has considered a marriage between her son and his daughter. In the context of the Fortinbras subplot, Polonius' name, which means "from Poland," is worth noting. Though a comic figure at whose bureaucratic doubletalk we are meant to laugh, he has a visibly sinister side as well, a penchant for political intrigue and spying. While his tactics are shady, his intentions are usually good, making him, like Claudius, a mixture of good and evil.

## Laertes

Polonius' son is one of several young men whose behavior is explicitly contrasted with Hamlet's. A courtier in training, he is not a politician like his father, but proud, hasty, sincere, and utterly devoted to fulfilling the demands of honor—traits that will sadly prove his undoing when he falls in with Claudius' plot. Apart from the implied running comparison with Hamlet, the chief interest of his character is the genuine intensity of his passion for the *outward forms* of honor. To get his sister a decent burial, for instance, he will openly quarrel with the priest; to avenge his father, he will violate the code of honor and even the dictates of his conscience with the poisoned weapon. In his own way he is an innocent like his sister, comparing himself at the end, as Polonius compared Ophelia at the start, to a game bird caught in a trap.

## Ophelia

Ophelia is Polonius' daughter. Her name is generally thought to be derived from the Greek word *apheleia*, meaning "innocence." This is certainly a good description of her outlook on life, every bit as ingenuous as her brother's. It may not, however, apply to her sexual activity: The intensity of her feeling for Hamlet suggests that something more than a flirtation has gone on between them, and the bawdy "St. Valentine's Day" song that she sings in her madness must have been learned somewhere, though its words should not be taken as literally describing the state of their relations. Some commentators have expressed shock at the coarse language Hamlet jokingly uses toward her in the Play Scene, but aristocratic manners were looser then, and it is really no worse than some of the interchanges between courtly lovers in Shakespeare's romantic comedies. Ophelia's meek reactions to Hamlet's language presumably come not from shock, but from confusion over his abrupt change of mood and attitude toward her since the Nunnery Scene. She of course has no idea of the state he is in, and it is possible that she thinks his condition has indeed been caused by her following her father's instructions and refusing to see him. Note that in the conflict between her love for Hamlet and her duty of obedience to her father's orders, she bows to Polonius' wishes. Hamlet is less obedient to the orders of the ghost, his father.

## Horatio

Hamlet's trusted friend Horatio is a gentleman and a scholar, but he is not of the nobility, since he appears to have no position at court except in relation to the prince. Hamlet's much-quoted tribute to him before the Play Scene ("Give me that man/That is not passion's slave") points up the balanced nature of Horatio's personality, precisely the quality Hamlet himself lacks. Of course, Horatio is also not forced to undergo any experience as intense as those that Hamlet suffers through. In his moderation of temperament, as in his intermediate rank, he represents the Renaissance version of the ancient classical ideal, the man fortunate enough to live without either excessive joy or suffering in his life. His vaguely Roman name and his Roman-style attempt to join Hamlet in death at the end confirm this.

## Rosencrantz and Guildenstern

Hamlet's two fellow students from Wittenberg are unmistakably members of the Danish nobility, and noticeably frivolous students compared to the serious Horatio. (The life Polonius fears Laertes may be leading in Paris probably has some similarity to theirs in Wittenberg.) Their names, which mean "wreath of roses" and "golden star," are authentic touches of local color, since both belong to aristocratic Danish families still in existence today. (Tradition, as usual unverifiable, says that two Danish nobles so named actually were sent on a mission to England in the late sixteenth century.) They are certainly courtiers skilled at politicking, and we learn enough from their evasion at their first meeting with Hamlet to justify his being suspicious of them. Whether they deserve to be put to death, however, is debatable, since they can have no idea of the king's true motives in employing them. On the other hand, the fact that they meddle in the business of kings and princes without questioning motives is a comment on their lack of principle, and Hamlet, in telling Horatio of their impending deaths, does not hesitate to draw the moral (*Act V, Scene ii, lines 62–68*).

## Fortinbras

The prince of Norway is a conventional, correct, ambitious military man, yet he is more an image in the play's structure than an individual personality. Fortinbras' chief role is to remind you, in the sphere of politics and kingship, of what Hamlet is not, just as Laertes does in the realm of family honor. Fortinbras figures in the play three times: at the beginning, when Horatio and, later, Claudius discuss his actions; in the middle, when Hamlet meets his troops; and at the very end. Like Hamlet, Fortinbras is the nephew of a reigning king, who is physically weak as Hamlet's uncle is morally weak. The throne of Norway being occupied, he seeks conquests elsewhere, never questioning their value. When he assumes the throne, he reverses the military victory that was the great triumph of King Hamlet's life. Fortinbras displays his inability to understand Hamlet when he orders a military funeral for him and declares that Hamlet would have made an excellent king. (He couldn't possibly know this; in any case, it's not likely to be true, at least not by Fortinbras' own standards.) In short, Fortinbras' soldierlike ability to ignore the moral complexity of life is a sort of saving grace for him. He is aptly summed up in his name, French for "strong-of-arm."

## Marcellus, Barnardo, and Francisco

The three soldiers of the Danish King's Guard are all ordinary, honest men, all suffering in their own way from the sight of the ghost, and from the mysterious air of gloom that has settled on Denmark with King Hamlet's death. Marcellus is apparently of slightly higher rank than Francisco and Barnardo (also spelled Bernardo); he is on sociable terms with Hamlet and up to date on his whereabouts. Both he and Barnardo are articulate officers of an elite guard rather than common soldiers. Barnardo is more bluntly straightforward but not less intelligent. Marcellus' belief in ghosts, like his religious faith, is balanced against his honest practicality. His assumption that there is a logical reason for every phenomenon makes him similar in character to the captain of Fortinbras' army, who speaks bluntly to Hamlet about the valuelessness of the land they are marching to conquer; possibly the same actor played both parts.

## Clowns

The two characters usually—and mistakenly—designated as "First and Second Gravedigger" are a comedy act, the company's resident low comedian and his straight man, identified in early editions of the play as "Clown" and "Other." Although in many Elizabethan plays the material performed by clowns is irrelevant to and detachable from the story (since they traditionally "worked up" their own material), Shakespeare always took unusual pains to make them an organic part of the larger work. The role he creates here for the clown is a comic contradiction in terms— a cheerful gravedigger. His robust good spirits, talkativeness, and a love of argument are all amusingly inappropriate to the cemetery where he works, and are balanced by his democratically stoic sense that everyone is equal because we all come to the same end. Isn't that exactly how you might expect human life to look from a gravedigger's point of view? This simple workingman's philosophy is elegantly balanced, at exactly the right point in the action, against the complexity of Hamlet's soul-searching. The gravedigger's companion, though often erroneously played as an apprentice or younger work partner, is a warden or church official in charge of the placement of graves in the churchyard. He does not argue with the clown for the simple reason that, as he is finally forced to admit, he agrees with him.

## The Players

Typically for professionals at work, these actors say virtually nothing that is not connected with their job, and are resolutely uninvolved with the events at court. What you learn from them is chiefly how Hamlet feels about them. As you might expect from a prince who is himself the hero of a play (at a time when the growth of Puritanism was causing constant protest against the dangerous influence of theaters in London), Hamlet is an enthusiast and a friend, one who believes deeply in the theater's importance to society and who has many objections to performers who don't live up to his high ideals for the art. From Hamlet's friendly greeting, especially as contrasted with his reserve toward Rosencrantz and Guildenstern, you can see that Hamlet is extremely fond of this particular company of actors; he is an aficionado of their less successful plays and twice addresses the player king as "old friend."

## Osric, Reynaldo, Voltemand, and Cornelius

Being a noble in attendance at a Renaissance court meant a variety of things. It meant a formal skill at elegant conversation, bearing, and dress; training in such gentlemanly activities as riding and swordsmanship on the one hand, music and writing poetry on the other. It meant the ability to use these skills in the service of the king, on matters ranging from international diplomacy to minor errands about the court such as the errand on which Osric is sent to Hamlet. And it meant the cunning to use the same skills for one's own advancement in the royal favor, which could mean titles, decorations, and large grants of land or sums of money if one were successful. Osric is a courtier who is preoccupied with formal behavior. It is clear from Hamlet's comments, and from Osric's failure to perceive that he is being mocked, that he is little more than a foppish, gesticulating fool. (Compare his manner to the dignified bearing of the anonymous lord who comes to Hamlet immediately after Osric has left; the lord carries out his mission with a minimum of fuss in barely a quarter of the time it takes Osric to deliver a simple challenge to a fencing match.) Some critics have tried to read into Osric's presence the notion that Claudius' court is pretentious and decadent, but this is an exaggeration of both his foppishness and his importance. Courtiers were under no obligation to behave elegantly; they were members of a hereditary aristocracy and largely did as they pleased, which is precisely why displays of elegant manners and fine speaking were so valued by monarchs. Consequently, every court had its Osrics, and they turn up regularly in Elizabethan plays. It could more likely be considered a measure of Claudius' good sense that he confined the trivial Osric to domestic errands and sent a reliable, well-spoken man like Voltemand on ambassadorial missions. From Voltemand's brief report on his meeting with the king of Norway you can infer that he (and presumably the silent Cornelius as well) is an efficient, intelligent person of dignified bearing, just the sort a king can trust to get the business done. You get a glimpse of how such a man is molded, and of the kinds of backstairs business he might have to meddle in, from the little scene between Polonius and Reynaldo (presumably a young courtier in training). While sending him on a simple errand to bring money and letters to Laertes in Paris, Polonius teaches the boy to find out how Laertes is behaving by spreading mild slanders about him. Reynaldo is an alert and eager student.

## Priest

Stage tradition has made this "churlish priest" an unpleasant character. What his two brief speeches portray is a somewhat snobbish professional, compelled under political pressure to perform a task he regards as distasteful and improper. The only surprising part is that he is so outspoken in the presence of the king and queen, possibly from a wish to underline the extent to which he is protected by the church from their taking action against him.

# Other Elements

## SETTING

Because the Elizabethan theater used little or no scenery, the sense of place in a Shakespeare play changes as the characters enter and leave the stage. Where it is important, Shakespeare always indicates the time and place of the scene through a line of dialogue (as in the first scene, "Tis now struck twelve.") or through a formal device like the fanfares that announce the entrance of the king and his court. The fact that the story takes place in Denmark in the twelfth century mattered very little to Shakespeare and his audience; the tradition of reproducing a historical period with realistic accuracy on the stage did not come into being till nearly two hundred years later. Elizabethan costumes were as lavish and expensive as could be, but they were the costumes of Shakespeare's own time, whether the play was set in ancient Rome or medieval England. The image of Denmark is mainly communicated to the audience by Shakespeare's using the cliché that the Danes were heavy drinkers, which is one reason he so strongly emphasizes Hamlet's dislike for Claudius' drinking habits. The world was just beginning to be mapped at this time, and a London audience probably had only the vaguest notion where Denmark was located: Shakespeare himself was so uninformed he confused *Dansk*, the Danish word for Denmark, with the Baltic seaport of Gdańsk or Danzig, at that time a free city-state, which is how he came to the mistaken idea that Denmark shared a common border with Poland. All this proves that Shakespeare's plays are set "in the mind's eye," in an imaginary world of their own, which is yours to conceive as you choose, within the limits of the play.

## THEMES

### Justice and Revenge

All the action of *Hamlet* is based on the one task the ghost sets the prince: to avenge his father's murder. This powerful demand is countered in Hamlet's mind by three questions: Is revenge a good or an evil act? Is Claudius truly guilty and so to be punished? Is it Hamlet's responsibility to punish him? Throughout the play Shakespeare raises questions about whether justice is to be left to the state or taken into one's own hands, and about whether it is possible, in a cunning and deceitful world, to tell the good man from the criminal. These questions are focused on Hamlet, who must decide whether to avenge his father or not, and if so, how. They are reflected in the parallel stories of Fortinbras and Laertes, who also have obligations of revenge to fulfill.

### Destiny and the Purpose of Life

Linked to the theme of revenge is the great question of Hamlet's inner meditations: Is there a point to life at all? Do we suffer in this harsh world for a purpose, or simply because we are afraid to find out what may lie beyond it? And if there is a higher, universal force guiding each of us in a certain direction, how do we learn what it is so that we can accept its guidance? Much of Hamlet's anguish is caused by his effort to link even the most trivial event to the order of the

universe. Is he right in doing so? And does he suc-
ceed—does life finally reveal its meaning to him?

## Madness and Sanity

The question of Hamlet's sanity is openly discussed
in the play and has been a subject of debate for centuries. Is Hamlet really mad? If so, what causes Hamlet's madness? Is it his reluctance to take revenge? Is it
his confused feelings about his mother? Is he in fact
sane and the world mad for failing to understand the
things he says? Is he sometimes pretending to be mad
and at other times genuinely unbalanced? Remember,
the play gives another example of madness in Ophelia, and you should ask some of the same questions
about her.

## Appearance and Reality

Allied to the question of Hamlet's madness is a variety of references to the idea of acting a part or of presenting a false image to the world. Hamlet demands
honesty, but is he himself always honest? Many other
characters, at various times, seem to be playing parts,
and the troupe of players is in the play as an active
reminder that in real life a person can play many roles,
and it is not always easy to tell what is true from what
only appears to be true. At the very center of the play
is Hamlet's view of acting on the stage, expressed in
his advice to the players. You can compare it with the
picture Shakespeare gives of Hamlet, and the other
characters, acting in their "real" lives.

## Women

Hamlet's views on women are complex and
intensely emotional. The only two women characters
in the play are the two who are most deeply attached

to him—his mother and Ophelia, the young girl he loves. Why is his bitterness toward his mother so strong? What are the various feelings that go into his changing attitude toward Ophelia? As you study the play scene by scene, you'll see to what extent the two women's responses bear out the truth of his accusations, and to what extent they do not.

## Rights and Duties of Kingship

Shakespearean tragedy often turns on the question of who is to be king—on who is best qualified to accept both the privileges and the responsibilities of rule. As you read *Hamlet*, keep in mind these questions: What are the obligations of a king to his people? Who in *Hamlet* has the most right to be king? Who is most qualified to be king? Is an honest king necessarily the best king? Is a peaceful king better than a warlike one? How much say should the public have in choosing a king, and how much the nobility? In the scene-by-scene discussion we'll also take a look at what being king means to each of the four characters who claim the Danish throne—Claudius, Hamlet, Laertes, and Fortinbras—and how well each one would rule.

## Poison and Corruption

Corruption, rot, disease, and poison are among the chief sources of poetic imagery in *Hamlet*. The poison with which Claudius kills King Hamlet spreads in a sense through the entire country till "something is rotten in Denmark." Look for examples of this imagery as you go through the play. Is the arrival of Fortinbras at the end meant to be a cure? If so, what sort of cure will it be?

# STYLE

The language of Shakespeare's plays tends to frighten many students and put them off. This comes from being told Shakespeare's plays are great poetry. To get around this, always remember that for Shakespeare's audience poetry was a kind of game, a way of marking in words the difference between a play and real life.

For Elizabethans, the poetic imagery and feeling of the great speeches in *Hamlet* had the excitement that a big song number in a musical comedy or a rock concert has for us. Like music, poetry is a way of heightening the power of what is being said in a play. It does this with sound and rhythm, with images, and, in Elizabethan verse, with what we call rhetoric. Rhetoric was taught to educated people in Shakespeare's time through the study of the Latin poets and orators. An Elizabethan gentleman was expected to be able to indulge in this elegant form of showing-off, and a gift for it was a way of gaining recognition at court or in the theater. Courtiers took for granted that flights of rhetoric would be part of any play they went to see, and ordinary people enjoyed it as something special and outside their daily experience. Shakespeare first became famous for his great rhetorical gift: You can see it in *Hamlet* when he makes Hamlet say he loved Ophelia more than forty thousand brothers could, or when he makes his mother compare the pictures of his father and Claudius.

Closely tied up with rhetoric as a field of study for the Elizabethans was logic, or the art of thinking in sequence. It is especially important in *Hamlet* because the hero is a student of philosophy, which means he has been learning how to express ideas in logical form. Sometimes Shakespeare uses logic to show

Hamlet's sense of humor, as when he "proves" that Claudius is his mother. At other times he builds, out of the textbook ideas of logic, the great soliloquies in which Hamlet meditates on the purpose of life and death. In fact, the line "To be or not to be: that is the question," though the most famous in the play, is not original with Shakespeare; he is making Hamlet quote the opening of the standard philosophic debate on whether life is worth living. What is important, of course, is that these elements are always used in a human and individual way. *Hamlet* is a story about people and their lives, not a textbook discussion of abstract ideas.

At the time it was written, Shakespeare was just beginning to develop the innovative approach of what we think of as his late style, in which the smooth and conventional rhetoric of his earlier plays is chopped up and fragmented to reflect the inner rhythms of a human mind, and not the polish of a system of writing in which all the characters think alike. When Hamlet bandies words with Osric or Polonius, or makes fun of Claudius' proclamations, Shakespeare is ridiculing the conventions of rhetoric; and in the soliloquies, with their jumps from one thought to the next, he develops a lean and disturbing poetry that has made the play seem alive to every century.

## POINT OF VIEW

The main thing to remember about *Hamlet*, as about any play, is that it is not a novel, in which the story is seen through the eyes of the author or the character who narrates. A play is told by having the characters present their opposing points of view in conflict with each other. We call the sum total of what these represent, when the action is completed, the author's vision. The great challenge of writing a play, which Shakespeare met more brilliantly than any writer who ever lived, is to make each character seem to take on an independent existence, with his own motives and his own approach to life, and yet have all these independent entities add up to one thing.

Because Shakespeare's sense of life was so broad and inclusive, many people have complained over the centuries that he does not tell his readers how to view the characters: Is Hamlet mad or sane, good or evil? Is it right for him to keep postponing his revenge? Are Claudius' tactics justified? Do Rosencrantz and Guildenstern deserve to be put to death? In a general sense, Shakespeare answers all these questions for the audience of his own time by never directly attacking the standard beliefs of an ordinary Elizabethan theatergoer. Because his artistry is so great, however, his characters are so strongly individualized that their actions can be interpreted many different ways, like the actions of real people, whose motives we can never fully understand. As a result, there is no one interpretation, no permanently fixed point of view to a play like *Hamlet*; its beauty is bound up with the fact that it can mean so many different things to people and be understood in so many different ways.

## ELIZABETHAN ENGLISH

All languages change. Differences in pronunciation and word choice are apparent even between parents and their children. If language differences can appear in one generation, imagine how different the English Shakespeare used some four hundred years ago will be from the English you use today. Here is some information on Shakespeare's language that should make *Hamlet* a little easier for you to understand.

Adjectives, nouns, and verbs were more adaptable in Shakespeare's day. Nouns were often used as verbs. For instance, here "shark" is used as a verb:

> young Fortinbras, . . .
> Hath in the skirts of Norway, here and there,
> Sharked up a list of lawless resolutes
> *(Act I, Scene i, lines 108–11)*

Later, in Act III, Scene ii, line 13, the proper noun "Herod" is used as a verb: "It out-herods Herod."

Adjectives could be used as adverbs. In Act II, Scene ii, line 45, Claudius says: "Thou still has been the father of good news," using "still" where you would use "always."

Verbs could be used as nouns:

> You shall do marvell's wisely, good Reynaldo,
> Before you visit him, to make inquire
> Of his behavior.
> *(Act II, Scene i, lines 3–5)*

There "inquire" is a noun—you would instead say "inquiry." Also, instead of "marvell's" in line 3, you would today say "marvelously."

Many of the words in Shakespeare still exist today, but their meanings have changed. The change may be small, as in the case of "modesty," which meant "moderation," as in:

> Suit the action to the word, the word to the action; with this special observance, that you o'erstep not the modesty of nature.
> *(Act III, Scene ii, lines 17–19)*

Or the change may be important. For instance, "disposition" meant "behavior," "doubt" meant "strongly suspect," "it likes us" meant "it pleases us," "hams" meant "thighs," "wax" meant "grow," and "complexion" meant "appearance."

Words not only change their meanings, they are often discarded from the language altogether. The following words used in *Hamlet* are no longer current in English, but you can usually figure out their meaning from the context in which they occur (and in any case, most editions of the play contain a glossary of unfamiliar words):

**parle** *(Act I, Scene i, line 62)*: conference

**impress** *(I, i, 75)*: forced labor

**precurse** *(I, i, 121)*: omen

**suppliance** *(I, iii, 9)*: pastime

**clepe** *(I, iv, 19)*: call, name

**cerements** *(I, iv, 48)*: clothes for the grave, shrouds

**soft** *(I, v, 58)*: wait

**pioner** *(I, v, 163)*: miner

**bespeak** *(II, ii, 140)*: speak to

**fay** *((II, ii, 265)*: faith

**coted** *(II, ii, 317)*: overtook

**escoted** *(II, ii, 345)*: paid for

**tarre** *(II, ii, 353)*: provoke

**God wot** *(II, ii, 416)*: God knows

**quietus** *(III, i, 74)*: release from life

**fardels** *(III, i, 75)*: heavy burdens

**orisons** *(III, i, 88)*: prayers

**haply** *(III, i, 171)*: perhaps

**belike** *(III, ii, 137*: it seems, perhaps

**ventages** *(III, ii, 357)*: finger-holes in a musical instrument

**reechy** *(III, iv, 184)*: dirty

**ore** *(IV, i, 25)*: gold

**larded** *(IV, v, 38)*: highly decorated

**sith** *(IV, vii, 3)*: since

**simples** *(IV, vii, 144)*: medicinal herbs, herbal remedies

**kibe** *(V, i, 141)*: sore
**splenitive** *(V, i, 261)*: hot-headed
**poniards** *(V, ii, 149)*: daggers

Shakespearean verb forms differ from modern usage in two main ways:

**1.** Questions and negatives could be formed without using "do" or "did," as when Hamlet asks "Hold you the watch tonight?" *(Act I, Scene ii, line 240)* where today you would say "Do you stand watch tonight?"; or where Laertes states "O, fear me not!" *(Act I, Scene iii, line 55)* where instead you would say "Do not fear for me" or "Do not be anxious about me." Shakespeare could also reverse the word order in a sentence. He might say "What think you?" instead of "What do you think?" or "It looks not like him" instead of "It doesn't look like him."
**2.** A number of past participles and past tense forms are used that are considered ungrammatical today. For instance, "writ" for "written," "bed-rid" for "bed-ridden," "hap" for "happen," and "shook" for "shaken."

Shakespeare and his contemporaries had an extra pronoun, "thou," which could be used in addressing one's equal or social inferior. Frequently a person in power used "thou" to a subordinate but was addressed "you" in return, as when Hamlet and Horatio speak in Act III, Scene ii:

> *Horatio:*  Here, sweet lord, at your service.
> *Hamlet:*  Horatio, thou art e'en as just a man
> As e'er my conversation coped withal.
> *(lines 53-55)*

"You" was obligatory if more than one person was addressed, as in Act II, Scene ii:

> Welcome, dear Rosencrantz and Guildenstern.
> Moreover that we much did long to see you, . . .
> *(lines 1-2)*

but it was also used to indicate respect, as in Act I, Scene ii, when Laertes wants his father's permission to return to France:

>                         My dread lord,
> Your leave and favor to return to France
> *(lines 52–53)*

One further peculiarity of pronouns is important. When Claudius first appears in the play he uses the royal "we" to emphasize his right to the kingship:

> Though yet of Hamlet our dear brother's death
> The memory be green, and that it us befitted
> To bear our hearts in grief and our whole
>     kingdom . . .
> *(Act I, Scene ii, lines 1–3)*

Prepositions were less standardized in Elizabethan English than they are today, and so you find several uses in *Hamlet* that you would modify in your contemporary speech. Among them are "on" for "of," in

> What think you on't?
> *(Act I, Scene i, line 66)*

"of" for "from," in

> That, being of so young days brought up with
>     him
> *(Act II, Scene ii, line 11)*

"after" for "according to," in

> Use every man after his desert
> *(Act II, Scene ii, lines 536–37)*

and "of" for "between," in

> Since my dear soul was mistress of her choice
> And could of men distinguish
> *(Act III, Scene ii, lines 64–65)*

Contemporary English allows only one negative per statement and regards such utterances as "I haven't none" as incorrect. But Shakespeare often used two or more negatives for emphasis, as when Hamlet instructs the players: "Nor do not saw the air too much" *(Act III, Scene ii, line 4)*, and adds: "Be not too tame neither" *(line 16)*.

## SOURCES

Shakespeare did not invent the story of *Hamlet*. In fact, Shakespeare made up almost none of his own plots. That sort of originality was not considered important in his day; what his contemporaries admired was an improved version of what had been done before. So Shakespeare, like the other poets and playwrights of the Renaissance, adapted his plots from history, or from popular stories of the day.

In the case of *Hamlet*, Shakespeare made use of a story that had first appeared in the twelfth-century *Historiae Danicae*, or *History of the Danes*, by Saxo Grammaticus, and was popularized in a sixteenth-century French tale. The French version was certainly known to Shakespeare, since it was one of Francois de Belleforest's series of "tragic tales" *(Histoires Tragiques)* a work that also provided Shakespeare with the plots for *Romeo and Juliet* and *Othello*. Belleforest's version, with a Hamlet who feigns madness to escape the tyranny of his uncle, escapes to England where he marries the king's daughter, slaughters the entire Danish court on his return by setting fire to the hall, and finally chops off his uncle's head, is a good bit cruder than Shakespeare's.

In addition, another Elizabethan play about Hamlet appeared not long before Shakespeare's. We know about it through various references made at the time, but the play itself has disappeared completely, eclipsed by Shakespeare's enormously popular version. It may have been written by Thomas Kyd, author of the popular *The Spanish Tragedy*, and is referred to by modern scholars as the *Ur-Hamlet* (original version of *Hamlet*).

Both *Hamlet*s belong to a type of play, very popular in Shakespeare's day, known as the Revenge Tragedy. These plays trace their ancestry back to the ancient Roman tragedies of Seneca. Many of the elements in Hamlet—the murdered father, the ghostly apparitions, the mad scene, the bloody finale with the stage strewn with corpses—are common to this genre. However, the depth of the characterizations, the complexity of the ideas, and the beauty of the poetry found in *Hamlet* belong to Shakespeare alone.

One last curious coincidence concerns a play, *Antonio's Revenge*, by John Marston, that appeared around the same time as Shakespeare's. This shares many devices with *Hamlet* and was once thought to have been a source of material for Shakespeare. It is now generally assumed, however, that Shakespeare came first and that Marston, who uses similar effects with less coherent purpose, was simply copying a better writer—another sign of *Hamlet*'s tremendous and instantaneous popularity.

*Hamlet* appears to have been written and produced sometime in 1600 or 1601, roughly the midpoint of Shakespeare's career. We can date it this way because of the reference in Act II, Scene ii, to the players suffering from the competition of the "little eyases" of the children's acting company at the Blackfriars Theater, which began its residence there in the fall of 1600.

Also, in 1598 Francis Meres published a book called *Palladis Tamia, Wit's Treasury*, in which he praised Shakespeare as "most excellent" among English poets, and gave a list of his finest plays—a list that does not include *Hamlet*, which would certainly have been on it if it had been performed by that time. The Stationers' Register, a legal record kept for copyright purposes, records the impending publication of *Hamlet* on July 26, 1602. Thus, it is safe to say the play was written sometime between 1598 and 1602, and probably in 1600-01.

## FORM AND STRUCTURE

Elizabethan plays in general were loosely structured. They adapted the basic five-act form of ancient Roman tragedy, which had been revived by Italian scholars of the early Renaissance and brought back to London by English aristocrats traveling in Italy, to the needs of a commercial and popular theater.

The basic elements of a revenge tragedy were very simple. There had to be a *hero*, who had been violently wronged and was justified in seeking revenge. His *revenge* had to be aimed at an opponent, or antagonist, equal to him in power and in cunning, or the play would degenerate into a mindless series of victories for the superhero, and so become monotonous. The action had to be carried on in an *atmosphere* of gloom and terror, preferably with supernatural elements. A *woman the hero loved* had to be involved in the action, if possible as an innocent obstacle to his achieving his goal of revenge. And there had to be a *counterplot* (or subplot), started by the antagonist to defend himself, which would engulf the hero just as his vengeance was accomplished. In that way the hero would achieve what has come to be called "poetic justice" on earth, and at the same time be punished by Heaven for his sin of committing murder.

You can see that this simple structure is still very much with us in the violence of movies, television, and comic books. One reason we consider *Hamlet* better than these popular entertainments is that Shakespeare made his own variation on the form, fulfilling all its demands and at the same time rising above it through his brilliant use of language and his creation of complex characters. By making his hero a philosopher who doubts and mocks himself every step of the way, Shakespeare is able to prolong the suspense and devote the first three acts to the question of whether Hamlet will or will not take revenge. When Hamlet finally takes a decisive action, at the end of Act III (where the structure is expected to rise to a climax), it turns out to be a fatal misstep. Instead of killing Claudius, Hamlet kills Polonius. This act engulfs him in the counterplot of Claudius and Laertes, which holds our attention until the play's violent end. Hamlet's hesitation allows Shakespeare to explore the meaning of revenge on both the philosophic and the psychological level, and to connect that act with the much larger question of the meaning of life.

To make sure we never forget that Hamlet's story is that of a father, mother, and son, Shakespeare contrasts it with the subplot of Polonius and his children. Both the plot and the subplot are fused together at the climactic moment when Hamlet kills Polonius. This act ultimately results in Hamlet's death at the hands of Laertes, another son avenging his father. And both stories are framed in the story of Fortinbras, who avenges *his* father's defeat at the hands of King Hamlet by taking over the Danish throne when Hamlet dies.

Shakespeare's superiority in such matters as moral and psychological subtlety is pointed up by his ability to contrast the way two characters respond to the same event or carry out the same action. Hamlet is so structured, for example, that we are forced to compare Hamlet's use of the play to entrap Claudius with Laertes's invasion of the palace with an angry mob; or Hamlet's confiding in Horatio with Claudius' efforts to manipulate Polonius. Shakespeare also uses the play's structure to contrast a character's behavior with what we know of his thoughts and feelings, or to show him behaving differently in different situations. For instance, compare Hamlet's speeches to the ghost with his conversation immediately afterward when Horatio and Marcellus find him; or compare Claudius' public behavior in Act IV, Scene iii, with his "Do it, England" soliloquy right after. Because Hamlet himself is a wit and a maker of ironies, Shakespeare often uses him to point up these contrasts verbally and so intensify them, just as his mordant jokes heighten the atmosphere of gloom rather than dispelling it. As you explore *Hamlet* in more and more detail, the way Shakespeare balances and arranges the elements of its story will become more visible to you—and more exciting as well, since very new facet of the structure you find will reveal another nuance of Shakespeare's vision, another aspect of the seemingly infinite range of his poetic mind.

## The Five-Act Structure

The main plot and subplot stories are both framed by the story of Fortinbras' avenging his father

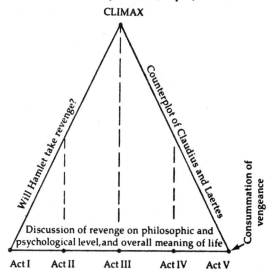

Hamlet discovers Claudius is guilty (main plot), but kills Polonious by mistake (subplot)

CLIMAX

Will Hamlet take revenge?

Counterplot of Claudius and Laertes

Consummation of vengeance

Discussion of revenge on philosophic and psychological level, and overall meaning of life

Act I     Act II     Act III     Act IV     Act V

**Act I: Exposition.** The rotten state of Denmark is disclosed, and the ghost appears with his call for vengeance.

**Act II: Rising Action.** Hamlet tries to discover the truth about the ghost's accusations.

**Act III: Climax.** Hamlet springs his "mousetrap" and catches his proof—Claudius is guilty.

**Act IV: Falling Action.** Claudius, not Hamlet, takes charge of events.

**Act V: Catastrophe.** The consummation of everyone's vengeance is achieved in a bloody ending that leaves only Horatio alive to tell the tale.

# The Play

## ACT I

### ACT I, SCENE I

The opening moments of *Hamlet* are among the most excitingly eerie in all drama. They establish at once the uneasiness, suspicion, and gloom that have pervaded Denmark since King Hamlet's death and Queen Gertrude's remarriage. The scene is the battlement or guard tower of Elsinore Castle at night. Barnardo, a guard, sees someone approaching, and calls out the customary challenge, "Who's there?" Barnardo is the relief guard, and the man actually on duty, Francisco, challenges him right back with, "Nay, answer me. Stand and unfold yourself." Barnardo identifies himself, and as they converse you learn that Francisco's watch has been uneventful ("Not a mouse stirring"), that it is after midnight on a "bitter cold" night, and that Francisco is "sick at heart" for reasons he does not explain.

---

**NOTE:** Almost every line in this tense, compact little exchange will have its echo later in the play. The confusion over who is on guard is like a miniature replica of the larger question: Who is ruling Denmark? "Long live the King!" is Barnardo's password, but the king is dead, and this irony hangs over the entire story. Francisco's heartsickness is another sign, the first of a series of references to sickness, disease, and corruption (the word literally means the rotting of flesh) that make up the play's most important pattern of images. Not only Francisco, but all of Denmark is sick.

---

The guards are joined by Barnardo's partner on duty, Marcellus, and by Horatio. Marcellus has invited Horatio to watch with them for the ghost they say they've seen twice. Horatio is skeptical, and sneers, "Tush, tush, 'twill not appear." They sit down while Barnardo launches into the story of how they saw the spirit last night, just as the clock struck one—and just as he says the words, the ghost appears, "In the same figure, like the King that's dead." Whether the ghost is a devil disguised as a dead man, or a spirit risen from the dead, is something you will have to wait to discover. Or is the ghost, as some critics have claimed, a mere hallucination, existing only in the minds of the characters? The ghost conveys by gesture that it has something to say, but when Horatio pleads with it to speak, it stalks away.

"Is not this something more than fantasy?" Barnardo asks, and the formerly skeptical Horatio is now forced to agree with Marcellus that there is indeed a ghost and that it does look like the late king—dressed as it is in the armor he wore in battle against Norway. In Horatio's opinion, this apparition "bodes some strange eruption to our state." This brings Marcellus to ask why the Danes are again making preparations for war. Horatio can tell him only what the rumor is: The late King Hamlet defeated Fortinbras of Norway and seized his lands. Young Fortinbras, hot-tempered like his father, is now scraping together a band of mercenaries to take back this fairly won territory. Marcellus thinks the ghost may be a good omen, but Horatio, who is "a scholar," reminds Marcellus that both earth and heaven showed omens of disaster in Rome before Julius Caesar's assassination:

> The graves stood tenantless and the sheeted
> dead

Did squeak and gibber in the Roman streets,

*(lines 128–29)*

As Horatio's speech comes to its climax of horror and foreboding, the ghost appears again, spreading its arms in an ominous gesture. This time Horatio is calmer, and he challenges the ghost to explain why it has appeared: for the sake of something left unfinished; to warn the country of approaching danger; or to point the way to buried treasure. Just as the ghost seems about to speak, a rooster crows, indicating that dawn is near, and the ghost vanishes. As the sun rises, Horatio proposes that young Hamlet, the dead king's son, be told about the ghost, because "This spirit, dumb to us, will speak to him." Marcellus agrees, adding that he knows exactly where the young prince will be.

---

**NOTE:**    Apart from its thrills and the beauty of its poetry, this scene is important for establishing the overall situation and particularly the character of Horatio, who will serve as a trusted friend and a sounding board for Hamlet all through the play. Think through the sequence of Horatio's actions and responses in the scene. Notice how he displays first skepticism, then fright, then bravery, then his knowledge of court affairs, then his education, and finally, in his description of dawn, his cultured eloquence. Notice also the way the play's story is magnified in importance as the scene goes on, like a photograph widening its perspective. What begins as the tension of two soldiers on a cold night has by the end of the scene broadened to include not only a whole nation, but also its place in the world. Shakespeare believed in a view of the universe that we now commonly refer to as the Great Chain of Being; in this view there is a natural order and harmony to life, and every living thing from the smallest insect up to the angels in heaven has a fixed place in it. If one element gets out of place, the chain is broken and the harmony disrupted; consequently, omens in the skies, or ghosts on earth, signal that some disruption is going on. After Horatio's speech about ancient Rome we are prepared for a series of images that will link night and omens to the story of Hamlet, and make an ongoing comparison between the distant, starry heavens and the squalid urgency of life on earth. The mention of Julius Caesar's assassination juxtaposed with the appearance of the ghost gives us a clue as to what this disruption may be. To cite one small example of the thoroughness with which Shakespeare prepares the way for his story, notice that Barnardo, telling Horatio the story, casually uses the phrase, "Let us once again assail your ears." You will very shortly learn of another character whose ears have been assailed, in a more dangerous and less metaphorical way, with tragic results.

## ACT I, SCENE II

From the battlements the action moves inside the castle, where the new king, Claudius, is addressing a council meeting. First he expresses regret over his "dear brother's" death, then announces that he has married the widowed queen, who sits beside him. He says that his councillors have supported him in this action, then goes on to discuss young Fortinbras, who has assumed that King Hamlet's death would leave Denmark vulnerable to attack. Claudius has written to Fortinbras' ailing and bedridden uncle, the king of

Norway, to put a stop to the young man's military activities. Voltemand and Cornelius are instructed to deliver the letter.

Claudius turns to Laertes. His tone becomes kindly and generous as he stresses how important Laertes' father, Polonius, is to him, and he agrees to grant the boy whatever he wants. What Laertes requests is permission to leave the court and return to France; his visit there had been interrupted by his return home for Claudius' coronation. After making sure that Polonius approves, Claudius grants Laertes his leave. He now turns to "my cousin Hamlet, and my son" and asks him, "How is it that the clouds still hang on you?" a reference to both Hamlet's moodiness and the fact that he is the only member of the court still in mourning for his father. The queen now speaks for the first time, adding her plea that Hamlet not "seek for thy noble father in the dust" forever. Since death is common to all, she asks, why does Hamlet seem to be making such a particular fuss about it? He replies that it is not a question of seeming, but being: His black mourning clothes are simply a true representation of his deep unhappiness.

Claudius chides the young prince for resisting the natural order of things. He reminds Hamlet that he is next in succession, and declares that he loves Hamlet as a father. Abruptly, he adds that Hamlet's desire to go back to his studies at the University of Wittenberg is against his, Claudius', wishes. The queen seconds this statement briefly and Hamlet, ignoring Claudius, replies, "I shall in all my best obey you, madam." The king seizes this moment to announce that he is delighted with Hamlet's willingness to agree. To honor him, every toast drunk at the royal banquet that night will be echoed by a salute from the castle's artillery. Claudius leads Gertrude away, and the court follows, leaving Hamlet alone.

Alone, Hamlet immediately launches into a violently emotional speech. He wishes he were dead, complains that suicide is a sin, describes the world as useless and disgusting. He then comes to the cause: his father's death. His father, compared to Claudius, was like a god next to something half man and half beast. His mother adored her husband—yet in a little over a month after his death she has married her husband's brother, "no more like my father/Than I to Hercules." Seeing someone come in, he calms down.

---

**NOTE:** This is the first of the soliloquies that allow you to hear Hamlet's innermost thoughts. At this point he is mostly preoccupied with his mother and with her remarriage; he spends very little time praising his late father. A disappointed idealist, he has no patience with the world, with himself, and particularly not with women. Soon you will see how his disappointment with his mother fortifies his distrust of Ophelia. Notice that Claudius, in attacking Hamlet for his grief, took pains to stress Hamlet's weak, unbalanced nature ("obstinate . . . unmanly . . . peevish"). Here, Hamlet apparently accepts this view, comparing himself ironically to the mythical strong man Hercules. Full of interrupted and unfinished sentences, the speech is obviously the outpouring of a man in a deep state of emotional distress and confusion. Whether his distress is justified, or merely the raving of an over-sensitive mind, is something you will have to decide as the play develops.

---

The people Hamlet has seen coming are Horatio, Marcellus, and Barnardo. He greets them politely, calling Horatio "my good friend" and asking why he has come back from Wittenberg. When Horatio says he came for Hamlet's father's funeral, Hamlet quips bitterly: "I think it was to see my mother's wedding." His joking leads him into a serious statement of his grief, and then to reminiscence, saying "My father—methinks I see my father." This startles Horatio, but gives him an opening for what he has come to tell Hamlet: "My lord, I think I saw him yesternight." Hamlet interrogates Horatio and the guards closely about the ghost, and then declares, "I will watch tonight," and

> If it assume my noble father's person
> I'll speak to it, though hell itself should gape . . . .
> *(lines 267–68)*

Hamlet sends them off, begging them to keep this a secret, and promising to meet them later on the platform where they stand guard. Alone, he briefly expresses his fear that his father has been the victim of foul play, and hopes he can stay calm till nighttime.

---

**NOTE:**      After the moaning distress of the soliloquy, Hamlet's behavior in this scene is something of a shock. He is poised, alert, articulate, and prepared for action; he seems to sense in advance what they have to tell him. Though cautious at first, he is apparently impressed by Horatio's scholarly objectivity and quickly opens up to him. Notice how symmetrically this scene is structured: First you see Hamlet at court with Claudius and his mother. Next you see him alone, pouring out his floods of melancholy. Then you see him with his friend Horatio and people he can trust. In the first and third sections of the scene his grief expresses itself in bitter mockery; in the middle section you see the melancholy that lies underneath it. You have now seen him matched up against nearly all of the play's major characters, and are fully aware of the range and depth of his emotions. His two decisions—to stay in Elsinore and to see the ghost—have set the two sides of the plot in motion. In his next scene he will meet the other character whose behavior has been puzzling, and the action will begin in earnest.

## ACT I, SCENE III

The next person we see, however, is Laertes, who is saying good-bye to his sister Ophelia as he prepares to sail back to France. What he is most concerned about is her relationship with Hamlet. He warns her not to trust the prince, not to expect that he will marry her (since reasons of state will probably match him with some foreign princess), and above all not to sacrifice her virginity to him. Ophelia straightforwardly promises to do what he says, and then saucily reminds him not to be a hypocrite, but to follow his own teaching. "O, fear me not!" Laertes begins, but breaks off the conversation sharply as Polonius comes in, amazed to find his son, to whom he has already said good-bye, still there. Having urged his son to hurry, Polonius now makes him listen to a lecture on how to behave like a man of honor and moderation. Some see this speech as the balanced advice of a moral and worldly gentleman; others see it as a series of cliches from a vain and pompous old man. After Laertes finally leaves, Polonius berates Ophelia for not resisting Hamlet's advances. When she protests that Hamlet "hath importuned me with love/In honorable fashion," he repeats Laertes' warnings, calling Hamlet's sacred vows "springes [snares] to catch woodcocks" and ordering Ophelia to stop seeing the prince. "I shall obey, my lord," she answers as they go off.

---

**NOTE:**     This is your first view of Ophelia, and you can see that her character has something in common with Hamlet's. She obeys her father, as he does his mother, and yet like Hamlet she evidently has some reservations about the principles on which that obedience is based.

Notice that when Laertes and Polonius describe Hamlet they could be talking about themselves: Laertes says Hamlet is hot-headed and easily swayed; Polonius, that Hamlet's vows are hypocritical. In terms of the play's overall imagery, note in Laertes' speech that on Hamlet's making a good marriage depends "the safety and health of the whole state," a reflection of the sickness theme.

Polonius' order to Ophelia not to see Hamlet, a decision made in suspicion and haste, will have serious consequences. The story of Polonius and his children is strictly speaking a subplot, but this is one of many actions that weld it to the main plot more strongly than any similar subplot in Shakespeare.

---

## ACT I, SCENE IV

On the guard platform in the cold midnight air Hamlet, Horatio, and Marcellus are waiting for the ghost. Trumpet fanfares and cannon shots offstage tell them that the king and his party are up late drinking. Hamlet hates the custom, which he says gives Danes the reputation of being drunkards. Just as he is pointing out that one flaw in a man's nature can destroy or corrupt all his virtues, the ghost appears. Exclaiming "Angels and ministers of grace defend us!" Hamlet approaches it, assuring his companions that he will find out whether it is a good or an evil spirit. He pleads with it to explain why his father's spirit should rise from its grave and walk the earth. In response, the ghost beckons him away, to speak with him alone. Horatio and Marcellus warn him not to go; it may tempt him to the edge of the battlements, where he will fall over. Hamlet shrugs off their objections, declaring that his life is of no value and his soul, being immortal, cannot be harmed. When they try to restrain him physically, he fights them off and leaves with the ghost.

## ACT I, SCENE V

Hamlet and the ghost re-enter from another direction, indicating that the scene has shifted to another part of the battlements. When Hamlet, unsure where the ghost is leading him, refuses to go on, the ghost speaks at last. Noting that he must walk the earth by night and suffer the tortures of hell during the day, he tells Hamlet that he is indeed his father's spirit, and that Hamlet must avenge his "foul and most unnatural murder." The murderer, he says, is none other than Claudius, who poured poison in the king's ear while he was asleep in an orchard. The official story is that he was bitten by a snake, but according to the ghost,

> The serpent that did sting thy father's life
> Now wears his crown.
>
> (lines 45–46)

Hamlet, who has suspected his uncle all along, exclaims, "O my prophetic soul!" The ghost goes on to describe how Claudius used his clever wit to seduce the queen, and how he himself felt at the moment when the poison took hold, with no oppor-

tunity for the last repentance necessary for a dying
Christian. Hamlet, he says, must not tolerate his
uncle's making the royal bed of Denmark "A couch
for luxury [lust] and damned incest"; however, he
must not take any action against his mother—"Leave
her to heaven" and to her own remorse. Since dawn is
breaking, the ghost is forced to leave. "Adieu, adieu,
adieu! Remember me," he says as he vanishes.

Hamlet is stunned. His worst fears have been real-
ized. Calling on heaven, earth, and hell, he vows to
erase everything but his father's story from his mind,
attacks his mother ("O most pernicious woman!"),
and can calm himself down only by writing in his
notebook his perception about his uncle—"That one
may smile, and smile, and be a villain." As he swears
again to remember his father, Hamlet is interrupted
by the shouting of Horatio and Marcellus, searching
for him. They naturally want to know what has happened, but Hamlet evades their questions. He will say
only that "It is an honest ghost," and then tries to
make them swear on his sword never to reveal what
they have seen. They are afraid to be trapped into an
oath instigated by an evil spirit. They refuse—they
have already sworn "by heaven" not to reveal it—and
their fears are confirmed by the ghost's voice com-
manding "Swear" three times from under the floor-
boards as they shift their ground. "This is wondrous
strange," exclaims Horatio, and Hamlet gives the
skeptic's view its final rebuke as he says:

> There are more things in heaven and earth,
> Horatio,
> Than are dreamt of in your philosophy.
>                                   (lines 191–92)

Hamlet warns his friend not to be surprised if he
appears to be mad and do strange things. Promising
to reward the guards as well as "so poor a man" can,

he again beseeches them to keep silent, adding,

> The time is out of joint. O cursed spite,
> That ever I was born to set it right!
>
> *(lines 215–16)*

Hamlet invites them to go in with him, and they all leave as day breaks and the first act ends.

---

**NOTE:**    Once again, in this scene, we can see the changeability of Hamlet's character. After the ghost vanishes he is utterly devoted to it; by the end of the scene he is already starting to regret his obligation ("O curse'd spite"). The question of whether Hamlet is mad or pretending to be mad (what is called his "antic disposition") has been debated for centuries; this scene suggests both possibilities. The ghost's revelation unbalances his already disturbed emotions, but by the time he gives his warning to Horatio he seems to be plotting to pretend madness in some way. Many of the things he says in later scenes will of course seem insane to those who don't know the truth, because from this point on Hamlet is a man with a secret and a mission. Using evidence from various parts of the play, you'll have to decide whether Hamlet merely feigns madness or whether he is in fact mad.

---

# ACT II

## ACT II, SCENE I

We know time has passed because Laertes has arrived in Paris and needs money. Polonius is sending a messenger, Reynaldo, with it, and instructs the young man before seeing Laertes not only to make inquiries about his son's behavior from other members of the Danish colony in France, but to disarm them into telling the truth by fabricating rumors of his own about Laertes' wild behavior. If they confirm the rumors, says Polonius, "Your bait of falsehood takes this carp of truth." Wordy and hedging in his instructions, the old man forgets the point he is making halfway through, so that Reynaldo has to prompt him.

As the messenger leaves, Ophelia comes in, deeply upset. Hamlet, whom she has been refusing to see, has invaded her room with a terrifying look on his face, grabbed her by the wrist, stared at her intensely, sighed, and then stalked out, still staring at her. Polonius, jumping to conclusions as usual, decides that Hamlet is truly in love with Ophelia after all, and that her refusal to see him has driven him mad. He takes her instantly to inform the king.

---

**NOTE:**    Is Hamlet play-acting, or showing signs of madness? Is he experiencing true melancholy or relishing his role as romantic hero? All these interpretations can be supported by the text. Some readers argue that Hamlet, deeply disturbed over the news of his mother's hasty remarriage, has now found that the other woman in his life is behaving strangely toward him. Given her father's close friendship with Claudius, he naturally worries that her unexpected coldness may be part of a plot against him. He would like to unburden himself to her, but he is stopped by both his promise and the fear that she might tell her father. Taken together, all these conflicting impulses produce in him an action that is, in effect, no action. You will see an expanded version of this later—this is only a warning sign—when Polonius plots a confrontation between Hamlet and his daughter.

Subplots in Shakespeare often echo the main plot in a comic way. Notice in this respect how Polonius' scene with Reynaldo continues the subject of pouring poison—in this case the poison of false gossip—into the ear.

## ACT II, SCENE II

A fanfare announces the arrival of the king and queen, greeting two new characters, Rosencrantz and Guildenstern, childhood friends of Hamlet's who have been summoned back in haste from Wittenberg to help discover what has changed Hamlet's behavior and to draw him into court amusements. The queen adds to Claudius' request the promise of a kingly reward. The two young men vow their obedience to the royal command and go off to see Hamlet.

In this and subsequent appearances by Rosencrantz and Guildenstern, you'll have to pay close attention to what they say and do to decide whether their actions are determined by their affection for Hamlet, their allegiance to the crown, or their desire for personal gain. Your interpretation will color your decision as to whether or not they deserve their fate.

Polonius comes in with two pieces of news: The ambassadors to Norway have returned, their mission successfully accomplished, and he has discovered the cause of Hamlet's lunacy. The king is eager to hear about the second matter, but Polonius persuades him to deal with the ambassadors first, and goes out to bring them in. The king repeats Polonius' words to Gertrude, who maintains the cause of Hamlet's moods is obvious: "His father's death and our o'er-hasty marriage." Polonius comes back in with Voltemand and Cornelius, the first of whom describes what has happened: The king of Norway was under the impression that Fortinbras' army planned to attack Poland. Learning the truth, he was furious to have his age and sickness taken advantage of, and

immediately sent out orders to stop Fortinbras, who
obediently apologized. This so touched the king that
he granted his nephew a reward of 3000 crowns a year
and ordered him to send his army against Poland
instead. Since they will need to cross Denmark to get
there, Norway requests Claudius to give them a safe-
conduct pass. Claudius is delighted at the success of
the mission, and promising to reach a decision later,
he dismisses the two ambassadors with thanks.

Polonius now launches into a long, doubletalk analysis of Hamlet's madness and its cause. He reads
aloud a love letter of Hamlet's to Ophelia, explains
how Ophelia came to him, what his response was,
and how Hamlet went mad from her refusal to see
him. The king and queen are struck by the possible
truth of this, and Polonius proposes a test: Hamlet
often walks for hours in the castle's main hallway,
reading. At one such time Polonius will send Ophelia
to meet him, while he and the king hide behind an
arras or tapestry to watch. "We will try it," says the
king. With apt timing, Hamlet now comes in, reading
a book, and Polonius sends the king and queen away
so he can talk to the young man alone.

From the ensuing conversation we see that Hamlet's witty sarcasm has gotten both more bitter and
more eccentric. He calls Polonius a "fishmonger"—a
slang word for a pimp—and warns him, harshly, that
his daughter may become pregnant. When Polonius
asks what he is reading, Hamlet pretends it is a satir-
ical portrait of old men, which is a cruel caricature of
Polonius himself. "Though this be madness," Polonius says to himself, "yet there is method in't."

Suggesting that Hamlet go to an inner room that
may be less drafty, he says, "Will you walk out of the
air, my lord?" and Hamlet, taking him with ironic lit-
eralness, asks, "Into my grave?" More than ever con-

vinced that this is the madness of unrequited love, Polonius takes his leave. As he departs, Hamlet audibly adds, "These tedious old fools."

---

**NOTE:**    This bitterly comic scene is the first in the play to be written in prose rather than blank verse, and the shift tells you that, in some sense, Hamlet is no longer a noble character, but a clown trading quips with a fool. Time has passed, and he has not kept his promise. Instead of plotting Claudius' death, he reads, paces, and thinks about his own death. But he can no more commit suicide than he can murder.

Note that Hamlet sees himself growing old and useless like Polonius. Under the pressure of his inactivity and distrust of everyone around him, his wit has turned hostile. The comparison of Ophelia's possible pregnancy to the sun breeding maggots in rotten meat (note the rottenness image again) is notably cruel, even as a way to shock Polonius. But this static situation will soon change.

---

As Polonius is leaving, he meets Rosencrantz and Guildenstern. The fact that he has to point Hamlet out to them suggests that either Hamlet is much changed or that they do not know him very well. Hamlet, however, greets them happily as "my excellent good friends" and immediately starts to banter with them, making sexual jokes about Fortune being "a strumpet" because of her arbitrariness. "The world's grown honest [virtuous]," Rosencrantz declares, and Hamlet replies, "Then is doomsday near! But your news is not true"—the first hint that he is suspicious of what they say. He questions their motives for visiting, asking why they have come "to prison" (since he is forbidden to travel, Denmark is literally a prison to him).

Rosencrantz suggests that it is Hamlet's "ambition" (to claim the throne) that makes it one, to which Hamlet replies that he is without ambitions but has "bad dreams." Hamlet asks them again why they have come to Elsinore, and after many evasions and guilty looks, Guildenstern finally admits, "My lord, we were sent for." Beginning with "I will tell you why," Hamlet launches into an extraordinary speech of alternate praise and dispraise of the universe, saying that nothing makes him happy any longer, that "this goodly frame, the earth" is no more to him than "a sterile promontory"; the heavens, "this majestical roof fretted with golden fire," only "a foul and pestilent congregation of vapors"; and man, "the paragon of animals," a "quintessence of dust." Although he goes into such detail about his changed view of life, he does not tell Rosencrantz and Guildenstern its cause, as he has Horatio (compare Act I, Scene ii, lines 183-95).

---

**NOTE:** Hamlet's long and poetic prose speech, one of the most famous in the play, is an expansion of his remark some lines earlier that "there is nothing either good or bad but thinking makes it so." It expresses in philosophical terms the core of his problem: He wants to believe in the order of the universe, the beauty of the world, and the innate goodness of man, but in light of what has happened to his parents, and, in turn, to Denmark, all values seem false, and life itself seems meaningless. The careful crafting of the speech suggests that this, not his revenge, is what he has been agonizing over; he has been behaving like a student of philosophy, not a prince with a mission of vengeance to carry out. If life has no apparent purpose, and is meaningless, why seek revenge?

Rosencrantz apparently laughs, either at the way Hamlet is going on or at a misinterpretation of his remark "Man delights not me," for Hamlet quickly adds, "nor woman neither." Rosencrantz protests that he did not mean to laugh at Hamlet and covers the awkward moment with a piece of news: He and Guildenstern passed a touring company of actors on the road. When Hamlet asks which company, Rosencrantz tells him they are his favorites, "the tragedians of the city," and goes on to explain that they are traveling because a new company of child actors has replaced them as the most popular entertainment in town. Though this seems preposterous to Hamlet, it does not surprise him.

---

**NOTE:** The rivalry between Shakespeare's company and the newly formed children's company at the Blackfriars Theater was a subject of topical interest to Elizabethan audiences. Hamlet sees the popularity of these child actors as evidence of the world's pursuit of the shallow and superficial. In Hamlet's mind, this pursuit is linked to the shifting of his mother's affections from his father to his uncle.

Throughout the play Hamlet shows an ongoing concern with acting as an aspect of human behavior. His idealism demands that people be true to their own nature. He genuinely tries to live by Polonius' advice, "To thine own self be true"; as early as Act I, Scene ii, he is trying to tell his mother that his grief is not a matter of acting, of posturing and costume. With the players soon to arrive, Hamlet's notion of true and false emotion is about to get mixed up with what is commonly called the paradox of acting—the idea that an actor has to create a genuine emotion onstage in order to make his audience know what the character is feeling. In Hamlet's eyes this is impossible, as the very definition of acting implies *pretending* to have an emotion. However, his uncle's behavior and his own mixed feelings about revenge and murder are constant reminders to him that emotions can be feigned in real life too, that in fact there are situations in which the pretense of actors is more "real" than the feelings people must often pretend to show in public; and it is the actors who will give him the clue to his next move. As you go through the play, be on the lookout for the varied situations in which Shakespeare shows or refers to people "acting" in real life, and notice how each relates to Hamlet and his dilemma.

A trumpet fanfare indicates the arrival of the acting company at the castle. Hamlet's greeting clearly shows that he is on friendly terms with them. As a preview of their performance, he requests a speech from a play he admires (significantly, one that was not a popular success). The speech is the story of the Trojan War as told by the surviving Trojan prince, Aeneas, to Dido, queen of Carthage. Hamlet chooses the section that tells how Aeneas' father, King Priam, was slaughtered in battle by the brutal Greek soldier Pyrrhus, while the city of Troy was being sacked and burned by the Greeks. Hamlet recites the first part of the speech, describing Pyrrhus, dressed in black and covered with the blood of his victims, searching for the old king.

The company's lead actor now takes over, and describes how Pyrrhus finds the brave but feeble old man, King Priam, and slaughters him remorselessly. "This is too long," Polonius interrupts, but Hamlet rather insultingly overrules him. The next part of the speech describes how Priam's wife, Hecuba, the queen of Troy, witnessed her husband's murder and mutilation, and how her wailing would have brought tears to the eyes of the gods.

At this point Polonius interrupts again, upset that the player has gotten so carried away that his face is flushed and he is crying real tears. Saying, "I'll have thee speak out the rest of this soon," Hamlet turns the actors over to Polonius to be housed and fed. As Polonius leads the actors off, Hamlet takes the first player aside and asks him to play *The Murder of Gonzago*, adding that he will give him an additional speech "of some dozen or sixteen lines" to insert in it. He sends the first player after Polonius, and says good night to Rosencrantz and Guildenstern, who leave.

Turning to the audience with the simple declaration, "Now I am alone," Hamlet launches into his second great soliloquy, "O, what a rogue and peasant slave am I!" He compares himself bitterly to the player, who could summon real passion and real tears for the story of Hecuba, a mythical character ("What's Hecuba to him, or he to Hecuba?"). He wonders what the player would do in his, Hamlet's, situation:

> Had he the motive and the cue for passion
> That I have? He would drown the stage with
>   tears . . .
> Make mad the guilty and appall the free [that is,
>   the innocent].

But I, Hamlet says, am a dull, daydreaming good for nothing, who can't even avenge a murdered king. No one has accused me of being a coward, but I would deserve it if they did; I must be a coward, or my uncle would long ago have been a corpse for the carrion crows to pick at. The fact that I stand here cursing this way, like a common servant, shows what an idiot I am.

Once these violent emotions roused by the player's speech have calmed down, Hamlet goes on to describe what he will do to remedy this situation: He will have the players perform a story that resembles the murder of his father, and he will carefully watch Claudius' reactions. If Claudius turns pale it will prove the ghost was telling the truth. This test is important to Hamlet, for it is still possible that the ghost may have been a devil, "and the devil hath power/T' assume a pleasing shape." The act ends with Hamlet declaring roundly:

> The play's the thing
> Wherein I'll catch the conscience of the King.

---

**NOTE:**     Though Hamlet's moods are always changing, you can see that his second soliloquy is different in its overall quality from his first. "O that this too too sullied flesh would melt" is all depression and sorrow. Now, the presence of the players sets off Hamlet's anger, first at himself and then, remembering his task, at Claudius ("Bloody, bawdy villain!/ Remorseless, treacherous, lecherous, kindless villain!"). The last third of the speech, triggered by his anger and his guilt at having delayed, is at last a practical step forward on Hamlet's part. The player's speech has given him a role model to emulate. Although the fact is never mentioned, Hamlet would of course know that Pyrrhus' attack on King Priam is revenge for the killing of Pyrrhus' father by Priam's son Hector. Pyrrhus is the archetype of the revenger. But can Hamlet be that violent, and cause Gertrude the grief Pyrrhus brings to Priam's wife, Hecuba?

Note that with the player's speech, and Hamlet's soliloquy after it, the play has returned to blank verse.

---

# ACT III

## ACT III, SCENE I

The king and queen are interrogating Rosencrantz
and Guildenstern to see what they have learned about
Hamlet's "turbulent and dangerous lunacy." (Ob-
serve that Claudius already thinks Hamlet is dangerous, though Hamlet has not yet given him any reason
to think so.) The young men report that Hamlet has
received them well, but that he evades them with "a
crafty madness" whenever they try to ask the cause of
his distraction. However, Hamlet was delighted to
hear about the players and has ordered them to perform tonight; the king and queen are invited. The
king urges them to keep pumping Hamlet for information, then dismisses them.

Claudius and Polonius have arranged to spy on a
meeting between Hamlet and Ophelia. The queen
leaves, hoping that Ophelia's beauty is the cause of
Hamlet's madness and that Ophelia's virtue may
make him sane again. Polonius has arranged for
Ophelia to walk along the corridor with a book as if
praying, adding that with "pious action we do sugar
o'er/The devil himself." This observation brings an
unexpected reaction from Claudius. In an "aside," a
speech to the audience that the other characters are
not meant to hear, he admits that Polonius' words
have stung his guilty conscience, and compares his
hypocritical behavior to a prostitute's heavily madeup
face. Polonius says, "I hear him coming," and the two
men go to their hiding place.

**NOTE:** Claudius' aside shows you two important things. First, that he is indeed guilty—that the ghost told the truth. Second, that he does have a conscience for Hamlet to "catch." The fact that Claudius is not a simple villain, that he is unhappy at having committed his crime, makes us look forward with excitement to what will happen in the play scene, but it also makes us less eager to see Hamlet's revenge. We can sympathize a little with Claudius now. Perhaps the fact that Claudius is a mixture of good and evil is the reason why a sensitive, philosophic man like Hamlet has trouble killing him.

The metaphor Claudius uses, comparing his false words to the paint on a harlot's cheek, is also significant, for it recalls Hamlet's feelings about makeup as part of the falsity of women. Remember in Hamlet's letter the reference to the "most beautified Ophelia"? This subject, a traditional target for moralists of the time, will come up again in a very short time, when Hamlet and Ophelia at last confront each other.

Hamlet comes in, and not finding whoever has sent for him, begins his third soliloquy, "To be, or not to be." Unlike either of his earlier inner-voice speeches, this one shows us his student mind at work. It is a philosophic debate, of a kind common in the period, on the subject of whether life is worth living. Is it "nobler" for a person to accept the miseries life brings him, or to fight against them and die? Dying is the problem, of course: We do not know what happens after death. It may be a peaceful sleep, but it may be a nightmare. It would be so simple to end all one's troubles by simply putting oneself to rest ("quietus") with a dagger ("a bare bodkin"), but men fear death—"the undiscovered country" from which "no traveller returns"—and consequently put up with familiar problems rather than "fly to others that we know not of." "Conscience" (awareness) thus makes "cowards of us all," for when we think about the consequences of an action, we end up not taking it. This is an important clue to Hamlet's character and the reasons for his delay. A man of thought rather than action, he sees the many sides of an issue, and ends up doing nothing. At this point Hamlet interrupts his train of thought because he sees Ophelia, apparently praying, and says to her, "Nymph, in thy orisons [morning prayers]/Be all my sins remembered."

---

**NOTE:** "To be, or not to be" is the most famous, most quoted, most parodied, and most overinterpreted piece of verse in the English language. A good way to appreciate it is by ignoring the many commentaries that turn it into a monument, and trying to work out its meaning for yourself. You will see that it deals with the most basic of all subjects—life and death—and is for the most part very straightforward in its logic. You can also see that it is not a "dramatic" speech; it analyzes a problem instead of deciding on a solution, expresses Hamlet's ideas rather than his feelings, and does not drive him on to any action, not even to the action of refusing to act. Its relation to the play is something like the eye of a hurricane, a still point at the center of a state of extreme turmoil, in which the themes of the story are examined in a calm and objective way. Its connections to Hamlet's character and situation are of course strong: He has been contemplating the prospect of killing himself; he has been ordered by the ghost to kill Claudius; he has told Rosencrantz and Guildenstern that he has "bad dreams"; the ghost has left him with a tangible and unpleasant picture of what the afterlife may be like; and finally, he has been more and more worried by his inability to act on his father's commands. In his soliloquy Hamlet is trying to search out, in a scholarly way, the basic thought process that will help him solve his problems. Significantly, he is distracted by Ophelia's arrival before he can come to any conclusion.

---

Ophelia and Hamlet greet each other rather formally. Ophelia increases the coolness between them by presenting Hamlet with the "remembrances" (presumably trinkets or love letters) he has sent her. Hamlet refuses to take them, saying, "I never gave you aught," a remark that must be interpreted in a nonliteral sense. Ophelia, in her straightforward way, flatly contradicts him—"you know right well you did"— and begs him to take his gifts back, as they are meaningless when the giver is unkind. This rattles Hamlet, who feels that it is Ophelia who has been unkind to him. Not realizing that she has been influenced by her father's and brother's view of his intentions, he begins badgering her, challenging her honesty, and claiming that her beauty has corrupted it. "I did love you once," he says, and her reply, "Indeed, my lord, you made me believe so," only goads him into cruelty. When he takes back the remark ("I loved you not") her modest reply ("I was the more deceived") produces a violent outburst of disgust with himself, her, all men and women, and the whole process of sex and procreation. Does it seem out of character for Hamlet to lie about his true feelings toward Ophelia? Is it possible that he never loved her? Is he trying to return some of the hurt she has caused him? Has his mother's incestuous marriage caused him to lose faith in love itself?

Wanting to believe in Ophelia's virtue, he repeatedly urges her to isolate herself from the world's corruption, including his, by going into a convent or nunnery. He interrupts his tirade abruptly with the question, "Where's your father?" which suggests he may know or suspect that he is being spied on. Ophelia's answer is a lie: "At home, my lord." It is the only reprehensible action we ever see her commit. Hamlet, however, does not challenge it, and continues railing at her, causing her to call on heaven to cure him, for she now genuinely believes he is insane. He curses her marital prospects, attacks her and all women for their makeup and flirtatious ways, and proclaims that marriage will be abolished. "Those that are married already—all but one—shall live," he says, which must confirm Claudius' worst suspicions about what is really upsetting Hamlet. Urging Ophelia once more to go "to a nunnery," Hamlet stalks off, leaving her to moan miserably about the difference between his former nobility and his present demented state, "Like sweet bells jangled, out of tune and harsh."

The king and Polonius come out of their hiding place and ignore Ophelia's distress as they discuss their observations of Hamlet. The king, now surely realizing that Hamlet knows his secret, insists the prince is not mad (though his talk "lacked form a little") but is dangerous. His solution is to send Hamlet to England to collect an unpaid tribute to the Danes. (What else he has in store for Hamlet we can only suspect.) Polonius agrees, though still insisting that love is at the core of Hamlet's grief. He at last turns to Ophelia, but only to tell her she does not need to report what Hamlet said, as they have heard it all. To the king he suggests withholding announcement of Hamlet's embassy to England till the next day. After

the play tonight, Polonius will arrange another inter-
view for Hamlet, this one with the queen:

> And I'll be placed, so please you, in the ear
> Of all their conference.

(lines 194–95)

If the queen cannot discover the cause of Hamlet's
grief, Polonius argues, then send him to England or
confine him "where/Your wisdom best shall think,"
presumably meaning a madhouse. As they leave, the
king piously agrees with the old man that "madness
in great ones must not unwatched go."

---

**NOTE:**      You can see here that Claudius, unlike
Hamlet, is able to take decisive action without revealing his motives or his feelings. He is able to do this in
part because he surrounds himself with gullible or
obedient people. Whatever Gertrude may think, she
registers no disagreement with his plans, while the
doddering Polonius is not likely to be suspicious. In
the previous act Hamlet warned Polonius not to let his
daughter walk in the sun, which is exactly what he
has done in this scene, and with distressing consequences. His plan to eavesdrop on Hamlet's meeting
with his mother will shortly prove even more disas-
trous.

---

## ACT III, SCENE II

Evening has come, and Hamlet is with the players
before their performance, explaining how he wants
the new speech he has written to be delivered. As
always, the point he wants to make leads him to give
what is virtually a lecture, this one on the whole art of
acting.

---

**NOTE:**      Hamlet's advice to the players is another section of the play that has become familiar through frequent quotation, partly because people assume it states Shakespeare's own views on acting and on the art of the theater. What he says, however, is also relevant to the dramatic situation. As a well-educated nobleman who strives for a classical balance in life, Hamlet wants the actors to be moderate and natural in their depiction of life, not exaggerated, yet not dull. In addition to intensifying your suspense about the speech he has written and about how the king will react to it, the passage reminds us that only in the fictional reality of art can Hamlet find the ordered universe he seeks, just as he can find the perfect image of a son's revenge or a queen's sorrow only in the mythical figures of Pyrrhus and Hecuba. He believes that the theater exists to "hold the mirror up to nature" and hopes that Claudius will see his evil nature reflected in that night's performance.

Notice the change in Hamlet's behavior from the last time you saw him, shouting his bitterness at Ophelia. With the players, who are not involved in his "real" life, Hamlet can be at ease and at his best, a prince reminding artists of the ideals their art is meant to uphold. You know he is not so calm with his family or Ophelia.

---

Polonius, Rosencrantz, and Guildenstern enter with the news that the king and queen—which in effect means the entire court—will join Hamlet in watching the play. Hamlet sends Rosencrantz and Guildenstern off to help the players prepare and calls for Horatio. He explains his scheme, since he is the only one Hamlet can trust and asks Horatio to join him in watching the king. Horatio promises that he will not let the king out of his sight during the performance.

---

**NOTE:** Hamlet's speech to Horatio shows you again that Horatio, unlike Hamlet, is a moderate man, neither rich nor poor, neither violent nor melancholy. Hamlet loves and envies Horatio for not being "passion's slave," a good description of how Hamlet must see himself in his frenzied moods.

---

A fanfare announces the king and queen's entrance, accompanied by courtiers and guards bearing torches. The king immediately asks how Hamlet "fares," and Hamlet, punning on the sense in which the word means "dines," answers that he "eats the air" (another pun, on "heir") as chameleons were thought to do, and that this is not a good way to feed capons—a hint that he suspects Claudius, in naming him successor, of stuffing him with promises the way a capon is fattened before being butchered. Claudius pretends not to understand what Hamlet means.

Polonius announces that he was thought of as a good actor in college, where he played Julius Caesar: "I was killed i' the Capitol," he says. "Brutus killed me." Hamlet's reply, making puns on "Brutus" and "Capitol," unwittingly prefigures the "brute part" he will play later that night, when Polonius will be killed in earnest.

Told that the players are ready, Hamlet looks for a place to sit. Gertrude asks him to sit with her, but he declines, probably because he would then be unable to watch Claudius. Instead he turns to Ophelia and engages her in a bantering conversation full of sexual double-entendres. Her reactions, cautious and deferential, suggest that his changed attitude has her com-

pletely dumbfounded. When she remarks that he is
"merry," however, he seems to become mad again,
and says:

> What should a man do but be merry? For look
> you how cheerfully my mother looks, and my
> father died within 's two hours [not two
> hours ago].
>
> (lines 124-26)

"Nay," Ophelia replies, " 'tis twice two months,"
provoking Hamlet to a cynical speech on how long a
man can hope his reputation will last after he dies.

Before anyone can respond to this, music
announces the play. The entertainment begins in the
customary fashion with a pantomime prologue or
dumb-show in which a king and queen embrace, the
king falls asleep, the queen leaves, and then another
man comes in, kisses the king's crown, and pours
poison in his ear. When the queen returns she finds
the king dead. She is consoled by courtiers, including
the poisoner, who courts her with gifts and finally
wins her. This prologue is in effect a brief summary of
the situation that will begin *The Murder of Gonzago*, a
play that would tell how the murderer is discovered
and punished. Its resemblance to the murder of King
Hamlet is obvious, but no one knows this except
Hamlet and Claudius. Claudius does not react to the
pantomime. Such stories were common enough, and
he may assume that its relationship to his own case is
just an unfortunate coincidence. In many stage productions, Claudius is inattentive, whispering to Gertrude and conducting business during the dumb-
show. However, it is quite possible that a man of
Claudius' hypocritical abilities could watch the dumb-
show and not let his reactions show. Ophelia is puzzled by it; when she asks what it means, Hamlet

answers, "mischief," adding, in a joke meant as a warning to Claudius, "The players cannot keep counsel; they'll tell all."

The player king and queen now act out their devotion in rhymed couplets that suggest an earlier and more primitive form of playwriting. Gonzago and his queen have been married thirty years, they tell us, and Gonzago is ailing. When he raises the subject of his queen's remarriage after he dies, she refuses to hear, cursing the whole idea:

> In second husband let me be accurst!
> None wed the second but who killed the first.
> *(lines 191–92)*

Hamlet murmurs that this is "wormwood," a bitter medicine. The player king warns the queen that vows are often broken when the situation that created them is gone, but she swears even more emphatically never to marry again. The king asks to be left alone, as he is sleepy, and she leaves him with gentle good wishes.

At this pause in the action Hamlet turns to his mother and asks her if she likes the play. "The lady doth protest too much," she answers, suggesting that she knows what is coming. Hamlet promises the queen will "keep her word," probably in a mocking tone, since Claudius asks Hamlet if he is sure the story has nothing offensive in it. Only "poison in jest," Hamlet replies. When Claudius asks the name of the play, Hamlet tells him it is *The Mousetrap*, based on an actual case in Vienna. It is an awful play, he says, but "free souls" like Claudius and himself can cope with it. The murderer Lucianus now enters—the central character, presumably played by the actor for whom Hamlet has written the new speech—and Hamlet identifies him as "nephew to the King," which equates him at one stroke with Claudius and with Hamlet himself. Lucianus describes the mixture of poisonous herbs he has created, and pours it into the ear of the sleeping player king. If this were not enough to upset Claudius by itself, Hamlet follows it with another few lines of mocking banter, ending with, "You shall see anon how the murderer gets the love of Gonzago's wife." This is too much for Claudius, and in one of the most electrifying moments in all theater the lines of the five major characters clatter on each other's heels in response to Claudius' reaction:

> *Ophelia:* The King rises.
> *Hamlet:* What, frighted with false fire?
> *Queen:* How fares my lord?
> *Polonius:* Give o'er [stop] the play.
> *King:* Give me some light! Away!
> (lines 277-81)

"Lights, lights, lights," everyone shouts, and in an instant Claudius, followed by the entire court, has vanished.

Only Hamlet and Horatio are left on stage. Hamlet could not be more delighted; he sings songs and jokes with Horatio about joining a theater company. "I'll take the ghost's word for a thousand pound," he declares, and calls for the theater's musicians to play their recorders. His celebration is interrupted by Rosencrantz and Guildenstern, who report to the buoyant prince that the king is "marvellous distempered [very upset]." "With drink?" Hamlet asks punningly. He is rebuked by Guildenstern for his "wild" jokes, and told that the queen has sent for him "in most great affliction of spirit." Hamlet, whose jokes have made it nearly impossible for the pair to deliver this message, answers with comic pomposity, "We shall obey, were she ten times our mother. Have you any further trade with us?" The aggrieved Rosencrantz reminds Hamlet, "You once did love me," and the prince, raising his hand in a mock oath, swears he still does. Why not tell a friend what makes you act this way? Rosencrantz pressures him. "I lack advancement," responds Hamlet, meaning both that he does not know how to act like a courtier, and that the way for him to raise his rank is blocked. How can that be, Rosencrantz goes on, when the king has named you his successor? Hamlet begins to cite the old proverb, "While the grass grows, the horse starves," but interrupts himself halfway through. You can argue that Hamlet is lying about his ambition to be king (in fact, he tells Guildenstern that lying is easy). Some readers, however, have argued that one of Hamlet's primary reasons for seeking to kill Claudius is to gain the crown for himself.

The players come in with their recorders or wooden flutes and Hamlet challenges Guildenstern to play one. "I cannot," Guildenstern says. "It is as easy as lying," says Hamlet, and demonstrates how the instrument is played. Hamlet knows that Guildenstern has been "playing" him (in other words, trying to manipulate him), and asks Guildenstern if he, Hamlet, is easier to play a tune on than a pipe. "Call me what instrument you will," says Hamlet, "though you fret me [a pun: "frets" are the finger-rests on stringed instruments], you cannot play upon me." For this, Rosencrantz and Guildenstern have no answer.

Is Hamlet right to be angry and feel betrayed by these two "friends"? Or should they be excused for putting their duty to their country ahead of friendship?

This awkward moment is cut short by Polonius coming in with another message: the queen wants to speak with Hamlet immediately. Hamlet shows

Rosencrantz and Guildenstern how easily a fool can be manipulated by making Polonius contradict himself. Then, dismissing them all, he delivers the briefest of his soliloquies, describing the "witching time of night" when he feels ready to "drink hot blood" and do things that would terrify daylight. Remembering that he must go to his mother, he reminds himself to be gentle with her:

> Let me be cruel, not unnatural;
> I will speak daggers to her, but use none.

He feels, however, that she deserves worse:

> My tongue and soul in this be hypocrites.

---

**NOTE:**    This scene takes place at the exact center of the play. Each section of it shows a new aspect of Hamlet's personality—the critic, the trusting friend, the court jester, the jubilant boy, the mocking satirist, and finally the revenger, tense but quietly determined. No wonder Hamlet fascinates the world—he seems to be a whole tribe of characters all by himself. He is now apparently at a dazzling peak: Claudius has been "convicted," Rosencrantz and Guildenstern have been put in their place, Polonius has been made a fool of, and the ghost has been vindicated. No one can question that Hamlet has accomplished something. But now moves are being taken against him, and he faces the difficult task of confronting his mother. The time is coming for the great test of his strength of will.

---

## ACT III, SCENE III

Claudius, now worried that he really is in danger, has decided to send Rosencrantz and Guildenstern with Hamlet to England. He orders them to prepare for the trip quickly. They agree, echoing his fears with pious phrases about how death or injury to a king is destructive to his country as well.

---

**NOTE:**      Rosencrantz and Guildenstern's speeches are good examples of what is called unconscious irony. They do not know that the phrases they use to flatter Claudius have a double meaning to him, since he is not a legitimate king. The evils they describe as resulting from a king's violent death are already happening in Denmark, and their words give a foretaste of how they, too, will suffer.

---

As they leave, Polonius comes in to announce that Hamlet is finally on his way to his mother's room, and that he will spy on him. As Claudius has wisely pointed out, mothers are partial to their sons, and someone more objective should be listening.

---

**NOTE:**      Balance, or symmetry, is important in the structure of a Shakespeare play. For example, this scene parodies Hamlet's scene with Horatio before they go to watch the play—the two scenes differ only in terms of the motives and the degree of honesty of the characters. The hero or protagonist must be challenged by an antagonist of equal strength, as Hamlet is by Claudius; and each must have a confidant, as Claudius has Polonius and Hamlet has Horatio. Shakespeare is never satisfied, though, with obvious symmetries, as we are about to see.

---

Polonius leaves, and Claudius unexpectedly throws himself on his knees and tries to pray. In a soliloquy with many similarities to Hamlet's outbursts, he confesses his guilt and says his crime has

"the primal eldest curse upon't,/A brother's murder!"
He cannot pray, though he would like to; he is
trapped in indecision. He knows he should repent,
but cannot while he is

> still possessed
> Of those effects for which I did the murder—
> My crown, mine own ambition, and my queen.
> *(lines 56–58)*

In this world wealth and power can make people
ignore a crime, but there is no "shuffling" [trickery] in
heaven. He therefore calls to the angels for help, and
kneels in silent prayer, hoping against hope that "All
may be well."

---

**NOTE:**    Claudius' soliloquy is one of the play's
great surprises, first because it reveals him as human
and pitiable; second because it points up his similarity
to Hamlet, even in the way they think. If you look
back at the "To be, or not to be" soliloquy you will see
that Hamlet describes the state that Claudius is in
now. Comparing their words, however, also makes
us aware of the differences between them. Claudius
has committed a hideous crime. He hesitates to atone
for it, however, because he is afraid of the consequences and reluctant to give up his comfortable position. Hamlet, on the other hand, has been hesitating
to commit a crime, even under the extreme pressure
of an order from his father's ghost. Now, at the
moment when Hamlet is finally convinced of the
heavenly justice of the act, Claudius is taking his first
step toward repentance. The play seems to be revers-
ing itself, turning upside down as if on an enormous
pivot. There's no telling what may happen next.

---

While Claudius tries to pray, Hamlet passes by on his way to his mother's room. He sees the king unarmed, kneeling, defenseless. Will he kill him? It is the perfect opportunity. He could kill Claudius "pat" [right now], he says, but a man killed in the act of praying will go to heaven, while Hamlet's father burns in hell—"This is hire and salary," Hamlet tells himself, "not revenge." No, Hamlet will put his sword back in its sheath and wait for a "more horrid" opportunity, when Claudius is drunk, or angry, or "in the incestuous pleasure of his bed," or in some other act "that has no relish of salvation in't." That way Claudius will go to hell where he belongs. Remembering that his mother is waiting impatiently, he leaves, with a last threat to Claudius.

Whether Hamlet truly seeks a "more horrid" revenge, or is simply finding an excuse for his inability to act, is an issue on which critics passionately disagree. You can find evidence for both interpretations.

---

**NOTE:**      Hamlet's speech has shocked many people over the years by its seeming cruelty and immorality. As a good Christian he should want to send people's souls to heaven. This objection, of course, misses the point. As a good Christian Hamlet does not want to murder Claudius at all; it was only a little while ago, in the Play Scene, that he was finally persuaded that the act of revenge is a just one. What he doesn't realize is that Fortune is playing a cruel joke on him: Claudius' prayer is not true prayer, since he will not show true repentance, and Hamlet's killing him now would certainly send him to hell by any Christian terms. He has let his great opportunity to

avenge his father go by, and he will never get a better
one.

---

Claudius, unaware of the danger he has just been
in, gets up from his prayer too late to see Hamlet pass
by. In the couplet that rounds off the scene he reaf-
firms that his attempt to pray has been false and
futile:

> My words fly up, my thoughts remain below;
> Words without thoughts never to heaven go.
> *(lines 100–01)*

## ACT III, SCENE IV

We now see Gertrude in her "closet," a small inner
chamber used as a dressing room or private office.
Polonius tells her that Hamlet is on his way, and lays
out firmly what the queen is to say to him: "his pranks
have been too broad to bear" and she has constantly
had to intercede with the king on his behalf. As they
hear Hamlet in the hall outside, Polonius hides, as he
has said he would, behind a tapestry or arras covering
the wall of the room. (Remember that electric light did
not exist then; the corners of a room lit only by candles
and torches were dark and made good hiding places.)
Hamlet comes in with a challenging, "Now, mother,
what's the matter," and the play's famous Closet
Scene begins.

Hamlet responds to each of his mother's attempts
to start the discussion with a stinging, angry come-
back. When she finally gives up trying to reason with
him herself, Hamlet takes the initiative. He tries to
force her to discuss her bad conscience rather than his
bad behavior, but his aggressiveness frightens her.
Thinking that her son is trying to murder her, Gertrude calls for help, a call echoed by Polonius behind

the arras. Seeing this unknown shape suddenly move, Hamlet leaps into action, draws his sword, and stabs the figure. "Is it the King?" he asks, and is shocked when he lifts the curtain and sees the dead Polonius' face. "O, what a rash and bloody deed is this!" the queen exclaims, and Hamlet, keeping to his purpose in spite of the shock, replies, "Almost as bad, good mother,/As kill a king, and marry with his brother." "As kill a king?" Gertrude repeats, and for many readers this is the moment in the story when it first dawns on her what Claudius has done.

You can use this scene as evidence that Hamlet has always been capable of revenge, but lacked the opportunity. You can also use it as evidence that Hamlet can only strike out blindly in anger, not deliberately in cold blood. The stabbing of Polonius may have less to do with revenge than with Hamlet's need to prove himself a man of action.

Hamlet makes Gertrude sit down and begins attacking her again for her remarriage. He takes out two pictures—probably miniature portraits of the kind worn in a locket—one of his father, and one of Claudius, and insists that she compare the two. He equates his father with the Greek gods, and Claudius with "a mildewed ear" that spoils a healthy corn plant. He criticizes Gertrude for not acting her age, and suggests that she may even be mad for showing such bad judgment. "O Hamlet, speak no more," the queen pleads, admitting her own feelings of guilt over the marriage; but Hamlet ignores her pleas to stop, saying she lives "stewed in corruption," and calling Claudius "a murderer and a villain." As his attack on Claudius reaches its climax an astonishing thing happens: The ghost appears. Hamlet's extravagant reaction upsets Gertrude even more, for she cannot see the spirit and now thinks her son is surely insane. The ghost tells Hamlet that he has nearly forgotten his task:

> This visitation
> Is but to whet thy almost blunted purpose.
> *(lines 125–26)*

Hamlet tries to make his mother see the ghost, but Gertrude sees nothing and insists again that Hamlet is mad and hallucinating. (Is he? Some have argued that the ghost exists only in Hamlet's mind.) Once again Hamlet begs her to confess and repent her sins, and to give up Claudius—at least to give up sleeping with him:

> but go not to my uncle's bed.
> Assume a virtue, if you have it not.
> *(lines 180–81)*

Hamlet tells his mother that he will be a dutiful son again when she repents:

> And when you are desirous to be blest,
> I'll blessing beg of you.
> *(lines 192–93)*

He says he will give the court a good explanation for Polonius' death, and notes that "worse remains behind" to be done.

"What shall I do?" the queen bursts out, and Hamlet again, with unpleasantly graphic details, urges her not to make love with Claudius. (You learn in this passage, incidentally, that the king calls Gertrude "his mouse," a phrase that gives additional meaning to Hamlet's calling the players' play *The Mousetrap*.) Suddenly, still thinking perhaps of his plot against Claudius, Hamlet asks if Gertrude knows he is being sent to England. She confirms what he has presumably heard as court gossip that evening, and he again vows to outsmart his enemies, promising to trust his schoolfellows as he would "adders fanged." With one last "Good night, mother," he drags the body out of the room, leaving the stricken and shattered Gertrude alone.

---

**NOTE:** The Closet Scene is the emotional peak of *Hamlet*, just as the Play Scene is the peak of its action. It marks a further step in Hamlet's move toward revenge, but it is a mistaken one that will soon have tragic consequences. Because a great deal happens in this short and emotionally charged scene, you may want to go over it slowly, point for point, asking yourself to what extent Hamlet is justified in each step he takes. Look at all his reactions to what the queen says, and her reactions to what he says and does. Add up which of his lines you think would and would not make Gertrude think her son is insane. Ask yourself why Hamlet keeps coming back to the question of his mother's marriage, why the ghost appears to him but not to Gertrude, and what he thinks he is doing at each point in the scene.

---

# ACT IV

## ACT IV, SCENE I

Hearing the queen's sighs and moans of grief, Claudius immediately comes to her. Hamlet, she tells him, is "mad as the sea and wind" during a storm, and has killed the "good old man" Polonius. "O heavy deed!" the king exclaims, adding instantly, "It had been so with us, had we been there [he uses the royal "we," meaning "I"]." Claudius worries that he will be blamed for Polonius' death since he should have kept "this mad young man" under restraint. The king calls

Rosencrantz and Guildenstern and orders them to find the prince so he can be shipped away to England that morning. In the meantime he will call a council meeting, so that any slanderous rumors coming from the murder will "miss our name/And hit the woundless air."

---

**NOTE:**    This short and succinct scene is one of the best for observing Claudius as a character. His decisiveness and his ability to see all sides of a situation—everything that makes him a good politician—are in evidence here. You can argue forcefully that he is a hypocrite whose only strong feelings are for himself. Notice, for instance, that he shows no concern for Polonius and his family. (If you want to see what he really thinks, compare a formal scene like Act I, Scene ii, lines 44-64 with this one.) On the other hand, Claudius has not until this moment spoken of killing Hamlet and you can argue that the King truly believes that Hamlet is mad and poses a threat to Denmark.

---

## ACT IV, SCENE II

Hamlet has just hidden Polonius' corpse when he hears Rosencrantz and Guildenstern calling him. They come in, followed by guards, and demand to know where the body is. He answers arrogantly that a king's son does not need to reply to the demands of "a sponge." When Rosencrantz reacts, Hamlet describes the way a servile courtier is like a sponge, and is greeted with a hostile, "I understand you not, my lord." "I am glad of it," says Hamlet, "a knavish speech sleeps in a foolish ear." After more repartee about the body, during which Hamlet shocks Guildenstern by asserting that "the King is a thing," Hamlet seems to allow them to take him prisoner, but then suddenly dashes off in the opposite direction, shouting "Hide fox, and all after," the beginning of a children's game similar to hide and seek.

## ACT IV, SCENE III

Claudius discusses the problem of Hamlet with his advisers. Hamlet must be restrained, but he is so popular with "the distracted multitude" that the matter must be handled delicately. His trip to England must appear like a project that has been planned for a long time.

Rosencrantz and Guildenstern arrive with the news that they have caught Hamlet but that he will not tell them where the corpse is. Hamlet is led in under guard and interrogated by the king. His usual jesting replies have, since he killed Polonius, been more and more focused on death. After discreetly suggesting that the king can go to hell, Hamlet gives a clue to where the corpse is and the king sends his attendants to search for the body. Hamlet tells them cheerfully, "He will stay till you come."

The king now informs Hamlet that he is being sent to England. Hamlet, with a show of mock innocence, agrees to go. He salutes the king as "dear mother," a title he proves by absurd logic to be correct. After Hamlet leaves, the king orders his men to make preparations at top speed. When they depart, Claudius rhetorically begs England to carry out his orders and kill Hamlet, as otherwise Claudius will know no peace. He compares Hamlet to a disease in his blood, of which he must be purged.

## ACT IV, SCENE IV

The sound of a drum and the entrance of an army tell you that the action is now near the Danish border, where Fortinbras is leading his men into battle against Poland. You see him for the first time, sending his captain to the palace to receive Claudius' promised permission to cross Danish territory. His seven terse lines show him to be responsible, gentlemanly, and skilled in military etiquette. As Fortinbras leaves, the captain meets Hamlet on the way to his ship. Hamlet stops to talk to him, and the plain-spoken captain, after identifying the Norwegian troops, says frankly that the land they are fighting over is worthless in all but name. "Why, then the Polack never will defend it," says Hamlet. But yes, replies the captain, the garrisons of troops are already there. The captain leaves, and Hamlet tells Rosencrantz, Guildenstern, and the boarding party that he will be along in a moment. In his final soliloquy Hamlet expresses his shame and amazement that others can act, when he himself cannot. That Fortinbras, a "delicate and tender prince," is ready to go to war "Even for an eggshell" gives him a kind of greatness, says Hamlet, for no quarrel is too small when honor is at stake. A man who does not do what is set down for him by fate is "A beast, no more." Hamlet who has infinite justification for his action, is shamed by Fortinbras' willingness to sacrifice twenty thousand men for a plot of land not large enough to bury them. "O, from this time forth," he concludes, "My thoughts be bloody, or be nothing worth!" As the soldiers march past in the opposite direction, Hamlet goes to board his ship for England.

**NOTE:**    In this final soliloquy you see the same reasoning side of Hamlet that you saw in his "To be, or not to be" speech. Yet a change has occurred. The

traumatic events that have led to his being shipped off
to England have awakened in Hamlet the realization
that there is no escape from his destiny. His philosophy, which has been on the side of life, survival, and
caution, now is used to justify bravery, war, and
deeds of blood. Not the least surprising thing about
Hamlet is that, almost alone among Shakespeare's
tragic heroes, he prepares to confront his fate with a
full knowledge of what it entails, and despite the fact
that he disagrees with it. Though the next few scenes
will take you away from Hamlet and from the fulfill-
ment of his destiny, you feel, with him, that a decision
has been made. At some point he must act. This last
view of Hamlet, decisive and at peace with himself, is
meant to stay in your mind as a prologue to the violence that is soon to come.

## ACT IV, SCENE V

At the court Horatio pleads with the queen to speak
with Ophelia, whose distracted and irrational speech
is arousing the townspeople's suspicions. The queen
reluctantly agrees, confiding to the audience in an
aside that her feelings of guilt make each bad turn of
events worse than it is. When Ophelia comes in it's
clear that she has gone out of her mind. Her hair is
down and she communicates only in snatches of folk
songs. The entrance of the king makes her change
from a mournful tune to a bawdy song about a
seduced virgin. When she leaves, the king orders
Horatio to follow and keep a close watch on her.

**NOTE:**     Shakespeare makes the story of Ophelia
imitate Hamlet's in the manner of traditional subplots.
But where Hamlet's madness is a matter of increased

consciousness combined with intentional deceit,
Ophelia's is actual madness, for her sayings and
songs have only the slightest bearing on the reality of
the moment, however logical their cause. Like Hamlet, she has been shocked by her father's murder and
what seems to be a lover's betrayal. It is hard to tell
whether she realizes how closely the murder and
betrayal are connected since, as you are about to
learn, Claudius has kept the circumstances of Polonius' death a secret.

---

As Ophelia goes out Claudius remarks that her
madness springs from her father's death. He dis-
counts love as the cause, just as he earlier discounted
it as a cause for Hamlet's madness. Claudius goes on
to list for Gertrude the sorrows that are coming upon
them now, "not single spies,/But in battalions": Polonius' murder; Hamlet's forced exile; rumor and distrust among the public due to the secrecy surrounding
Polonius' death and burial; Ophelia's madness; and,
worst of all, the secret return of her brother Laertes,
who is accusing Claudius of Polonius' murder.

Confirming Claudius' worst fears, a violent noise is
heard outside, and a messenger runs in to tell Claudius that Laertes has invaded the palace with a mob,
and overpowered the royal guard; the people are
shouting to have Laertes crowned their king. Another
noise, and the doors are broken down, revealing Laertes and his followers. Seeing the king, he orders the
others to stay outside and guard the door while he
confronts Claudius alone.

Laertes attacks the king violently, shouting "O thou
vile King, Give me my father!" The queen tries to hold
Laertes back, but Claudius, with a great show of kingly calm, tells her to let him go since the aura of divinity
that surrounds a king will keep him out of danger.

Laertes demands to know what has happened to his father, and vows revenge. Claudius quickly asks if he wants to avenge himself on his friends or his enemies. "None but his enemies," says Laertes, and the king seizes the moment to add that he is guiltless of Polonius' death, and is in fact deeply grieved at it. He is prevented from going into more detail by the sound of Ophelia singing outside.

"Let her come in," the king orders, and the sight of his sister in her insane state makes Laertes cry out, "O heat, dry up my brains!" As Laertes begins describing how her madness fuels his passion for revenge, she begins another funereal song and tries to teach it to the others. She completely fails to recognize her brother. She distributes flowers to them (it was traditional at funerals for mourners to scatter flowers on the grave), and, after one more song of death and burial, dashes out, leaving Laertes stricken.

The king takes advantage of Laertes' distraught state to say that he shares the young man's grief, and offers to explain the whole matter of Polonius' death to a panel of his wisest friends. Let them decide whether I'm guilty, says Claudius, and then I promise to help you satisfy your thirst for justice. Completely cowed, the revengeful boy follows him out.

---

**NOTE:** A comparison between Hamlet and Laertes is implied in this scene, in which Laertes comes close to achieving Hamlet's own goals—the death of Claudius and the crown of Denmark. But Laertes' violent, sincere but superficial character can no more accomplish this against the subtle Claudius than Hamlet could have. Laertes says he is prepared to "dare damnation" for the sake of his revenge—something Hamlet may not be prepared to do—but a few kind words from the king, and the sight of Ophelia,

completely deflect him and make him putty in the
royal hands. Notice how well prepared Claudius is for
him, and how delicate his tactics are. Since Gertrude
is in the room, Hamlet and his responsibility for Polonius' death are never mentioned. Using techniques
you have seen him use before, Claudius flatters Laertes and refers every question to a party of "wise
friends."

---

# ACT IV, SCENE VI

Horatio receives letters informing him that through
a twist of fate pirates have attacked Hamlet's ship and
captured only him, while letting the others sail for
England. The pirates have treated him well, Hamlet
writes, and he in return will be expected to do a good
turn for them, presumably in the form of a ransom or
a royal amnesty for piracies along the Danish coast.
He encloses a letter for the king, begs Horatio to hurry
to him, and adds that he has much to tell him, especially of Rosencrantz and Guildenstern. Horatio
rushes off to find his friend.

# ACT IV, SCENE VII

Meanwhile the king has told Laertes his version of
the murder of Polonius. Why then didn't the king
take action against Hamlet? Claudius gives two reasons: First, because the queen dotes on him, and she
is "conjunctive to my life and soul" (he describes this
condition, evasively, as "my virtue or my plague");
second, because the general public dotes on Hamlet
so that attacks on him are turned against the attacker.
The persistent Laertes vows revenge. The king is
about to reveal his own plot against Hamlet when a

messenger arrives with Hamlet's letters. Claudius reads aloud Hamlet's terse note, which says simply that he is back in Denmark "naked," and that he will explain everything when he sees Claudius tomorrow. The king is utterly puzzled by this, but Laertes is delighted, because he sees his revenge taking shape. The king proposes a scheme by which Laertes can kill Hamlet and have it look like an accident: A French gentleman who recently visited the Danish court has praised Laertes' skill at swordsmanship, which made Hamlet envious. The king will arrange a challenge match between the two, with buttoned foils (that is, fencing weapons with their points covered), and will arrange for Laertes to choose one with an exposed point, with which he will stab Hamlet. Laertes goes further: he will dip the point in a poison so deadly that Hamlet will die from the slightest scratch. For safety's sake the king has an alternate plan—if Laertes does not wound Hamlet, he will prepare a poisoned cup for the prince and propose a toast.

Their plotting is interrupted by a commotion outside. The queen comes in with terrible news: Ophelia has drowned while hanging garlands of wildflowers on the branches of a willow tree overlooking a nearby brook. A branch broke, and the mad girl allowed herself to be carried away by the current, floating and singing snatches of old songs till the weight of her wet clothing finally dragged her down "To muddy death." Laertes cannot control himself and staggers out, overcome with weeping. The king hurries after him, afraid that this unexpected turn of events will start Laertes raging again.

---

**NOTE:**     This scene lets you look at the character of Laertes close up in a variety of situations. First he is calm, listening objectively to the king's explanation;

then, with the arrival of Hamlet's letter, he becomes angry again; next he allows himself to be cowed and flattered by the king; and finally, when the queen arrives with the news of Ophelia's drowning, he reveals a real tenderness beneath all his cruelty and bravado. Like Hamlet, he is tender and loving but driven to rage by forces beyond his control. Seeing all these aspects of him helps you think of him as a worthy opponent for Hamlet, whom you now know he will be fighting in the play's fifth and final act.

---

# ACT V

## ACT V, SCENE I

The scene changes to the cemetery at Elsinore. The gravedigger and another man, presumably a church official of some kind, are debating whether Ophelia, whom they take to have committed suicide, is entitled to a Christian burial. The talkative gravedigger comically proves, in hashed legal language, that she does not "unless she drowned herself in her own defense." His crony reluctantly agrees that she would not be buried in holy ground if she were not a gentlewoman (that is, an aristocrat). The gravedigger duly finds it a shame that the aristocracy have more freedom to kill themselves than ordinary Christians. He then proves in what is obviously a comic "routine" that gravediggers are the oldest aristocracy. Gravediggers are also the best builders, he says, because the houses they make last till doomsday. He sends the other man out for a pot of liquor, and goes back to work, singing a comic song about youth and age.

**NOTE:** This brief comic routine in prose gives you a hint of the tension that is going to surround Ophelia's funeral, and sets the scene for it. Shakespeare's comic characters are often ridiculed for their ignorance—the gravedigger's attempt to shape a legal argument seems to belong to this category—but as the scene continues you will see that the young prince-philosopher has something to learn from the old workman, and that he is learning it at the most opportune moment.

Hamlet, passing by with Horatio, is amused at the notion of a gravedigger singing while he works. In his digging the gravedigger tosses up a skull from an earlier burial, and Hamlet begins imagining satirically what kind of person it might have belonged to. But whether it belonged to a politician, a courtier, a lawyer, or a landowner, the person's acquisitions did him little good in the end.

"Whose grave's this?" Hamlet asks, and the gravedigger jokingly says, "Mine, sir," to which Hamlet punningly answers that it must indeed be his, because he is lying in it. Hamlet learns that the grave is being dug not for a man or a woman, but for "one that was a woman, sir; but, rest her soul, she's dead." Hamlet is struck by the man's courtly gift for wordplay, and remarks to Horatio that for the last three years he has noticed peasants acting more and more like courtiers. But he finds out there are more serious reasons to link this peasant with the court: He became gravedigger here the same day King Hamlet defeated old Fortinbras—which was the same day young Hamlet was born. As Hamlet asks more questions about his own madness, the conversation degenerates into vaudeville punning ("How came he mad?" "With losing his wits." "Upon what ground?" "Why, here in Denmark.").

The gravedigger now brings up another skull, which he says has been there twenty-three years. It belonged to Yorick, the late king's court jester, who once poured a flask of wine on the gravedigger's head for a joke. Hamlet is deeply struck by this remembrance of a man who carried him piggy-back in his childhood. He picks up the skull and begins musing on man's mortality. Putting down the skull because of its stench of decay, he describes for Horatio how all the great leaders of the past must have turned to dirt in the grave; Alexander the Great might now be a stopper for a beer-barrel. Hamlet's morbid musings are cut short only by the sight of a funeral procession headed by Claudius.

---

**NOTE:**    You can now see that Shakespeare means the gravedigger to have a certain symbolic position in Hamlet's life. A full generation older, the gravedigger began his work the day Hamlet was born, which was also the day of the dead king's greatest victory. The gravedigger's cheerful acceptance both of his unpleasant occupation and of the nature of death and the inevitable changes time brings, stand in marked contrast to Hamlet's shock and bitter dismay.

---

What Hamlet has seen, though he does not realize it yet, is Ophelia's funeral procession, coming from the church to the grave that has just been dug for her. Because the circumstances of her death are suspiciously like suicide (Claudius has presumably kept her madness, like the death and burial of Polonius, a secret), she has been granted only the briefest of rites.

Hamlet immediately notes that the procession must belong to a suicide. As he points out Laertes to Horatio, the boy begins quarreling aggressively with the priest over the shortness of the ceremony. The priest resentfully replies that if it were not for political interference, she should have been buried in unsanctified ground. Laertes angrily answers that his sister will be a ministering angel when the "churlish priest" is howling in hell, and Hamlet learns for the first time whose burial this is. The queen, scattering flowers over the casket, says, "I hoped thou shouldst have been my Hamlet's wife." If she is sincere, Laertes and Polonius were wrong to deny Ophelia this hope, and you can argue that they were indirectly responsible for Ophelia's madness. Or you may argue that Gertrude is merely mouthing platitudes at Ophelia's funeral.

Laertes, extravagantly cursing Hamlet—the one "whose wicked deed" made Ophelia lose her mind— begs them to hold off burying her for a moment and jumps into the open grave to hold his dead sister once more in his arms. In the grave he begs with even more extravagance that they bury him with her. The excessiveness of Laertes' reaction annoys Hamlet, and he reveals himself to the mourners, shouting, "This is I, Hamlet the Dane." Laertes lunges for him, cursing, "The devil take thy soul" and they struggle as the others try to separate them.

The queen finally convinces Laertes to stop fighting. Hamlet, unaware of the circumstances surrounding Ophelia's death, asks Laertes why he is treating him this way, since "I loved you ever." He doesn't wait for an answer, however, since "The cat will mew, and dog will have his day"—a proverb suggesting both that he cannot stop Laertes, and that Laertes will ultimately be unable to stop him. The king asks

Horatio to take care of Hamlet, and leads Laertes away from the disrupted funeral. He begs Laertes to restrain himself till the dueling arrangements can be made.

---

**NOTE:** Once again Hamlet's idealism and his unstable nature have lost him the advantage that his surprise return to Denmark might have brought. He has made an enemy of Laertes, who by rights should have been his ally, and he has reinforced with an embarrassing public incident the general belief that he is mad. Yet his behavior is not unjustified. Laertes' exaggerated behavior is an affront to Hamlet's rational nature and to his love for Ophelia. His shock at learning she has killed herself helps explain his impulsive and aggressive behavior. Also, having been away at sea, he does not realize the extent to which he has caused Ophelia's death, or how deeply Claudius has involved Laertes in the plot against him. Some have seen Hamlet's actions as overcompensation for his own awareness of his guilt in Ophelia's death, but there is no actual proof of this in the text: He is genuinely startled by Laertes' unfriendly response.

---

## ACT V, SCENE II

Hamlet tells Horatio the story of his brief voyage with Rosencrantz and Guildenstern. For some reason he could not sleep on the ship and impulsively broke into their cabin and stole the papers the king had given them. What he found was a command to the English to cut his head off without delay. Painstakingly, Hamlet wrote out a new royal commission, urging the English to execute Rosencrantz and Guildenstern without even allowing them time to confess and be absolved. He replaced Claudius' order with the false one, and put it in their luggage. The next day came the fight with the pirate ship, and Guildenstern and Rosencrantz were sent to their death. Hamlet points out, perhaps a bit defensively, that they "did make love to this employment," and that it is their own fault for being small men meddling in affairs above their rank.

---

**NOTE:**     Hamlet's cruelty toward his two former friends has shocked many people, but would not have surprised an Elizabethan audience. Rosencrantz and Guildenstern allied themselves with the king when common sense and loyalty to a friend might (or perhaps should) have brought them to Hamlet's side. Hamlet may very well regret his action—he swears in the Recorder Scene that he still loves them—but there is no question that he, and his audience, saw his action as necessary, if painful.

---

Horatio is shocked by Claudius' deviousness. Hamlet recites a list of Claudius' crimes and asks Horatio if he does not agree that Hamlet is justified in avenging himself. Horatio warns that there will soon be a report from England on the death of Rosencrantz and Guildenstern. "The interim is mine," replies Hamlet, adding that in any case life is brief at best, lasting no longer than it takes to count "one." Changing the subject, he regrets having lost his temper with Laertes, and agrees to apologize to him.

A courtier named Osric now enters with a message from the king. Hamlet delays his delivering it by teasing him, as once he teased Polonius, making him agree first that it is cold, then that it is hot. Osric finally manages to convey that the king has six valuable horses, which he has wagered against six weapons imported from France that Hamlet can beat Laertes in a fencing match. Is Hamlet willing? Hamlet dryly responds that he will be walking in the hall; that if the king and Laertes choose to stop by, and the weapons are brought, he will do his best. Osric leaves, and Hamlet sardonically comments to Horatio that there are many like Osric about the court, who use elaborate stock phrases of which they hardly know the meaning, because they have "got the tune of the time" and the age dotes on them.

As if to point up the absurdity of Osric's speech, a well-spoken "Lord" arrives with two further messages for Hamlet: The king wants to know if he is ready immediately or needs more time; and the queen wants to make sure he apologizes to Laertes before the dueling starts. Hamlet is straightforward and dignified, answering that he is indeed ready, and that the queen is quite right.

---

**NOTE:**     The presence of this second lord demonstrates that Osric's appearance is not, as some have theorized, a sign that Claudius' court is "decadent" and overindulgent. More likely, Osric is an extreme example of the type of person Hamlet hates most—one who is false in speech and action. As Hamlet approaches his ultimate test, Fate has put in his path a cartoon figure who represents everything he despises. How out of place Hamlet seems in a court filled with such trivial and shallow people.

---

Horatio tells Hamlet that he will lose the match, but Hamlet doesn't think so—he has been practicing since Laertes went to France. Hamlet admits deep misgivings but passes them off as worries that "would perhaps trouble a woman." Horatio offers to delay the match by telling the king Hamlet is not ready, but Hamlet refuses. Everything, he says in one of the play's most beautiful and most often quoted speeches, is in the hands of providence, even (citing the Gospel of Matthew) the fall of a sparrow. In a thought that reminds us of his "To be, or not to be" speech, Hamlet adds that no man can know what he leaves behind on earth, so the leaving itself, in a sense, cannot matter.

---

**NOTE:**      Here at last you see Hamlet in a state of peace and readiness, accepting his fate. His own philosophy has merged with the gravedigger's, and he can now accept the world on its own terms, whatever it offers him. It is in this scene, when he accepts his destiny, that Hamlet actually becomes what is called a tragic hero, confronting openly and in full readiness both the evil in the world and the flaws in himself that make him mortal.

---

Trumpets and drums announce the arrival of the entire court, with attendants bringing a table on which the weapons for the match—daggers and the long, narrow fencing swords called foils—are laid out. The king ceremoniously makes Hamlet and Laertes shake hands, and Hamlet makes a public, gentlemanly, and sincere apology to Laertes. He calls his madness his enemy, and explains that if he has injured Laertes while mad, he himself is on the injured party's side. Laertes replies evasively that he is "satisfied in nature," but that his honor demands he follow precedent by fighting the duel. He promises, hypocritically, not to wrong Hamlet's offered love. "Give us the foils," calls Hamlet, and cheerfully

starts making witticisms about how he will be Laertes'
foil, since the other man's skill is greater than his own.
"You mock me, sir," says the suspicious Laertes, but
Hamlet swears his sincerity.

The king orders Osric to bring the foils, and the two
men test and choose them. Hamlet warns the king
that he is betting on the wrong man, but the king
denies it. Claudius orders cups of wine to be set out,
promising that if Hamlet scores the first or second hit,
the cannon will fire a salute and a toast will be drunk.
The king offers to toss in Hamlet's cup a jewel richer
than any in the Danish crown. Toasting to Hamlet's
health, he orders the match to begin.

Hamlet scores the first hit. Laertes wants to resume
immediately but the king insists on having the promised drink. The cannon sounds (we now see the custom Hamlet spoke of with distaste in the first act), and
the king drops the jewel (a "pearl" containing poison)
in the cup, and offers it to Hamlet. "I'll play this bout
first," says Hamlet, and they fight again. Hamlet
scores another hit, which Laertes concedes. "Our son
shall win," the king remarks jovially, as if that was
what he wanted, and the queen, noticing that Hamlet
is sweating and out of breath, gives him her handker-
chief to wipe his forehead. Picking up the poisoned
cup, she announces, "The Queen carouses to thy fortune, Hamlet." "Gertrude, do not drink," the king
exclaims, but she insists, ambiguously, "I will, my
lord; I pray you pardon me." (Is God or Fate punish-
ing her for her incestuous marriage? Does she take the
drink, knowing it to be poisoned, to atone for her
sin?) Laertes whispers to the distraught king that he
will hit Hamlet this time, and the king curtly replies,
"I do not think't."

In an aside Laertes confides to the audience that wounding Hamlet "is almost against my conscience"; he is beginning to feel remorse for joining the king's plot. Hamlet challenges him to fight again, accusing Laertes of holding back. They fight to a standstill, with neither scoring; then suddenly, breaking the rules, Laertes rushes at Hamlet and stabs him with the poisoned sword. Hamlet fights back, and in the scuffle the swords get switched. The king calls for someone to stop them, but it is too late, and Hamlet wounds Laertes.

---

**NOTE:**    It is unclear from the stage directions exactly how this is supposed to happen, but a double disarming with an exchange of weapons was a standard maneuver in fencing at that time.

---

The moment the king has dreaded has arrived. The queen, on whom the poisoned wine has finally taken effect, swoons. Laertes says that, like a game bird in its own trap, "I am justly killed with mine own treachery." Hamlet, ignoring his own wound, asks about the queen, and the king, still hoping to lie his way out of the tangle, says, "She swoons to see them bleed." But the queen, at last realizing her husband's villainy, shrieks out with her dying breath that the drink has poisoned her.

"O villainy! Ho! Let the door be locked. Treachery!" shouts Hamlet, giving orders as if at last he is king. His cry stimulates the dying Laertes to a full confession. He tells Hamlet that he has only half an hour to live, that the poisoned weapon is in his own hand, and that "the King's to blame." "Then, venom, to thy work," exclaims Hamlet, wounding the hated Claudius and at last accomplishing his appointed task.

The king, conniving to the end, calls his courtiers to his defense, saying, "I am but hurt," but Hamlet, accusing him of his crimes to his face ("incestuous, murd'rous, damned Dane"), forces him to drink the rest of the wine. The king dies, and Laertes, begging Hamlet's forgiveness, points out the justice of it, since Claudius himself made the poison. Forgiving Hamlet for his own and Polonius' death, Laertes dies.

As Hamlet himself dies, he tries to explain what has happened to the assembled court; but he gives up under the effect of the poison, and pleads instead with Horatio to "report me and my cause aright/To the unsatisfied." Horatio, declaring himself "more an antique Roman than a Dane," tries to drain the dregs from the poisoned cup, but Hamlet wrenches it out of his hands and begs his friend to restore the "wounded name" he would leave behind if there were no one alive to tell his story. "Absent thee from felicity awhile," Hamlet pleads, showing that he now equates death with happiness.

Suddenly shots and the noise of an army are heard outside. Osric explains that it is Fortinbras' troops returning triumphantly from Poland, saluting the newly arrived ambassadors from England. The poison has now nearly overcome Hamlet; he has only enough strength left to propose Fortinbras as the next king of Denmark. He begins asking Horatio to explain to Fortinbras what has happened, but breaks off a sentence he will not live to complete. He exclaims, "The rest is silence," and dies. "Now cracks a noble heart," Horatio declares (recalling Ophelia's "what a noble mind is here o'erthrown"), and speaks a gentle epitaph for Hamlet:

> Good night, sweet prince,
> And flights of angels sing thee to thy rest!
> *(lines 385–86)*

A drum announces the simultaneous entrance of Fortinbras and the ambassadors from England, all horrified at the sight of the carnage. Death, says Fortinbras, must be having a banquet to take so many princes at one time. An ambassador, announcing with naïve pride that the king's orders have been carried out and "Rosencrantz and Guildenstern are dead," wonders who will thank him for the news. Horatio remarks that Claudius, who never ordered their death, would have been the last to thank him. Asking the others to put the bodies on ceremonial display, Horatio promises to explain the whole story truthfully,

> Of carnal, bloody, and unnatural acts;
> Of accidental judgments, casual slaughters;
> Of deaths put on by cunning and forced cause.
> *(lines 411–13)*

Despite his sorrow and his eagerness to hear the story, Fortinbras loses no time in pointing out his "rights of memory" to this kingdom. Horatio wants to speak of that too, but later—for now, they must make a public proclamation before rumors run wild and there are more upheavals. Fortinbras orders his men to bear Hamlet "like a solider" and to have the cannon fire in honor of his memory. If Hamlet had been crowned king, says Fortinbras, he was likely "to have proved most royally." As the men bear the dead bodies away, Fortinbras describes the sight as more suited to a battlefield than a court. The play ends with a funeral march and cannon shots in the distance.

# A STEP BEYOND

# Tests and Answers

## TESTS

### Test 1

1. Polonius advises Laertes to ____
   A. be prudent about finances
   B. seek revenge when it is called for
   C. pursue his music studies in Paris

2. The soldiers are tense at the start of the play because ____
   I. they expect an imminent attack
   II. they have seen a ghost
   III. something is rotten in the state of Denmark
   A. I and II    B. I and III    C. II and III

3. An example of Claudius' effectiveness as a king is the ____
   A. manner in which he denies Hamlet's request to return to school
   B. way he uses the talents of Rosencrantz and Guildenstern
   C. mission of Cornelius and Voltemand

4. The play-within-the play is *not* known as ____
   A. *The Murder of Gonzago*
   B. *The Lady Doth Protest Too Much*
   C. *The Mousetrap*

5. Claudius does not punish Hamlet after the murder of Polonius because ____
   I. of his love for Hamlet's mother
   II. of his sensitivity toward Ophelia

   III. Hamlet is popular with the Danish
      people
   A. I and II    B. I and III    C. II and III

6. Laertes' special contribution to the plot to kill     \_\_\_\_\_
   Hamlet is the
   A. special unction he bought from a
      mountebank
   B. poison in the chalice
   C. unbated sword

7. Claudius is upset over the murder of Polonius     \_\_\_\_\_
   because
   A. the old man had been a lifelong friend
   B. he might have been the victim himself
   C. he fears Laertes' reaction

8. The action that softens our feelings somewhat     \_\_\_\_\_
   toward Claudius is his
   A. attempt to pray
   B. love for Gertrude
   C. kind behavior at Ophelia's funeral

9. The line that shows Hamlet's intuitive feeling     \_\_\_\_\_
   about his uncle is
   A. "I must be cruel only to be kind"
   B. "O, my prophetic soul"
   C. "Remorseless, treacherous, lecherous,
      kindless villain!"

10. "Good night, sweet prince" is spoken to     \_\_\_\_\_
   Hamlet by
   A. Queen Gertrude
   B. Laertes, just before he himself dies
   C. his friend, Horatio

11. Is Hamlet mad or sane? Discuss.

12. Why does Hamlet hesitate before taking revenge?

**13.** To what extent is Claudius a good king? Give examples.

**14.** Compare Laertes and Hamlet as characters, showing how their stories contrast with one another.

**15.** Discuss the different views taken of the ghost by Marcellus, Horatio, Hamlet. Explain which is revealed by the play to be most valid.

## Test 2

**1.** In which of these quotations do you find an         _____
example of irony?
   A. "My words fly up, my thoughts remain below.
      Words without thoughts never to heaven go."
   B. "Do not as some ungracious pastors do,
      Show me the steep and thorny way to heaven"
   C.                 "This visitation
      Is but to whet thy almost blunted purpose."

**2.** One situation in which Hamlet is contrasted         _____
with Laertes is underscored when Laertes says,
   A. "Cut his throat 'i th' church"
   B. "And keep you in the rear of your affection"
   C. "I am justly killed with mine own treachery."

**3.** "I am more an antique Roman than a Dane" is         _____
spoken by
   A. Horatio, when endeavoring to kill himself

B. Laertes, when demanding the truth from Claudius
C. Osric, when declaring his loyalty to the king

4. The impassioned performance of the Player King leads Hamlet to say, _____
   A. "What's Hecuba to him, or he to Hecuba That he should weep for her?"
   B. "How all occasions do inform against me And spur my dull revenge"
   C.      "O, from this time forth, My thoughts be bloody, or be nothing worth!"

5. "Rich gifts wax poor when givers prove unkind" is said by _____
   A. Queen Gertrude to her son
   B. Hamlet to Guildenstern
   C. Ophelia to Hamlet

6. Which of the following statements is true? _____
   A. Hamlet compared himself favorably to Fortinbras
   B. There is ample proof that Gertrude took part in her husband's murder
   C. Polonius sent Reynaldo to France to spy on Laertes

7. One thing that Hamlet does not complain about in his "To be, or not to be" soliloquy is the _____
   A. law's delay
   B. primrose path
   C. pangs of despised love

8. The priest is reluctant to participate in Ophelia's funeral because _____
   A. the ground was unsanctified
   B. he felt that she had committed suicide

C. she lacked prayers, shards, and flints

9. The significant thing about a heroic couplet \_\_\_\_\_
   such as "Foul deeds will rise,/Though all the
   earth o'erwhelm them to men's eyes" is that
   it
   A. indicates the end of a scene
   B. is an example of iambic pentameter
   C balances the blank verse

10. King Hamlet's death is attributed to a \_\_\_\_\_
    A. poisonous snake bite
    B. heart attack
    C. leprous distillment

11. Go through the many deaths in *Hamlet*. In what way is
    each brought on by the character himself or herself and
    so part of what is called poetic justice?

12. How does Hamlet's advice to the players relate to the
    theme and action of *Hamlet*.

13. What does Hamlet learn from the gravedigger?

14. How does the First Player's "Hecuba" speech reinforce
    the themes of the play?

15. "Tragedy," wrote the critic Eric Bentley, "is extraordi-
    narily dependent on comedy." Discuss what he meant
    by this, and cite five examples of it in *Hamlet*.

## ANSWERS

### Test 1

| 1. A | 2. A | 3. C | 4. B | 5. B | 6. A |
|------|------|------|------|------|------|
| 7. B | 8. A | 9. B | 10. C | | |

   **11.** Hamlet is a complex and ambiguous character, and
his madness comes in two forms: One is the emotional over-
reaction that results from the shock of his situation; the other is the pretended madness of double-meaning puns and
seeming irrelevancies he employs in his dealings with Clau-

dius and Polonius. These two are closely bound up together. For instance, the fact that he is under severe emotional stress in his first scene with Claudius and the court (Act I, Scene ii) is made clear by the violent soliloquy that follows immediately afterward. On the other hand, people have often explained the emotional violence of his scene with Ophelia by suggesting that he knows their meeting is being watched by the King and Polonius. Because of Hamlet's complex and unstable nature, every reader must decide for himself at what points in the play Hamlet truly is or is not mad.

**12.** Many answers have been offered to this question: Psychologists believe with Ernest Jones that Hamlet's unconscious "Oedipal" desire to kill his father and marry his mother prevents him through guilt from killing Claudius. Nineteenth-century critics who saw in Hamlet an over-imaginative, idealistic poet-philosopher concluded that he had too weak a hold on reality to achieve his revenge; others have maintained that the act itself was against his religious or philosophic principles. In contrast, there has always been a school of thought that holds that Hamlet, in a complex position and faced with a clever and suspicious opponent, was in fact striving actively to accomplish the difficult task of killing a heavily guarded king, but lacked the opportunity. In this interpretation the key scene is that in which Hamlet kills Polonius, thinking it may be the king; here he does not hesitate. Those who disagree point out that Claudius' Prayer Scene is clearly meant by Shakespeare to be a turning point and a test of Hamlet's will. On the other hand, an Elizabethan audience would have understood the hero's reluctance to kill a man at prayer, though some later critics have found it "barbaric" for him to plan Claudius' damnation. Since this question is at the heart of Hamlet's "mystery," it is too ambiguous for any one answer to be correct.

**13.**   Shakespeare's genius is nowhere shown better than in his decision to make a complex and fascinating character out of the hero's opponent—a man who could be (and is in other Shakespeare plays) no more than a superficial, stock villain with no traits other than his evil. Claudius, in his scenes with the court and with Laertes, repeatedly shows his tact and judiciousness, his skill at dealing with people, and his desire to keep Denmark at peace and on good terms with its neighbors. Though he hardly conveys deep feeling for Gertrude, he also never treats her with less than husbandly respect. It is only the knowledge of his guilt and the fear of his crime being found out that drives him to evil and vindictive measures. In the Prayer Scene he begins to repent and refrains only from fear of punishment. Because of his unpardonable crime, he must ultimately be punished, but there is no question that Shakespeare meant us to regard him as a man in whom good and evil are mixed, and who might have lived a noble life if not for his criminal act.

**14.**   Though fundamentally honorable, Laertes has been misled by his "politic" father, Polonius, into believing that the most important part of honor is its outward form. For Hamlet, a philosopher who pursues the life of the mind, only the inner truth can bring a man to peace with himself. Consequently, while Hamlet struggles with his own soul but is for the most part good-humored and charming with others, Laertes often reveals a hot temper and a peremptory and cynical arrogance. Raised to distrust everything but outward show, Laertes cannot believe in anyone else's good motives. He will not believe Hamlet's love for Ophelia is serious (though both Hamlet and the queen confirm it later); he quarrels with the priest over the funeral; and he refuses to accept Hamlet's apology before the fatal duel. At the same time, because his anger is superficial, he is easily led by a hypocrite like Claudius into a conspiracy—something which Hamlet would never have done in his position.

**15.** Before the ghost appears, Horatio, as an educated skeptic, sees it as a "fantasy" or hallucination of the guards. Barnardo suggests that it is a good omen—the late king's spirit is protecting Denmark, which must arm again for war. Horatio, on the contrary, draws precedents from Roman history to show that it is an omen of evil. Both Marcellus and Horatio fear that it may be an evil spirit intending to damn or destroy Hamlet. Hamlet himself seems to toy with this idea at times; however, he accepts the ghost's story, at first cautiously and then unquestioningly after the Play Scene. At the same time, though, he disregards its instructions, provoking its appearance in his mother's room, which appears to calm him and help him accept his destiny. By the end of the play, there is no question that the ghost was speaking the truth. Whether its advice was good and heaven-sent, however, is unclear, considering the death and destruction to which its desire for revenge has led.

## Test 2

1. A     2. A     3. A     4. A     5. C     6. C
7. B     8. B     9. A     10. A

**11.** The murder of Polonius, though perhaps an excessive punishment for his eavesdropping, is the inevitable outgrowth of his spying on behalf of a king whose moral purposes he never questions. Similarly, Hamlet's execution of Rosencrantz and Guildenstern is warranted by their having put themselves so trustingly in Claudius' hands. Laertes and Claudius, as the former points out, are fittingly caught in their own trap, and the queen's poisoning is a logical result of her having trusted, despite her better judgment, in a marriage she knows to be incestuous. Hamlet's own death, finally, is the tragic result of his having postponed his revenge till he is caught up in the circumstances of Claudius' counterplot; he is in a sense sacrificed to his responsibilities. In addition, he is expiating his murder of Polonius. Only Ophelia's drowning while insane seems an excessive punishment for the comparatively minor sins of trusting her father and telling Hamlet one small lie in the Nunnery Scene. On the other hand, Shakespeare is at pains to examine the danger the world holds out for those who trust too innocently to others' motives. Ophelia trusts her father and brother blindly, as they trust Claudius, and like them she is destroyed.

**12.** Hamlet's description of the naturalism, balance, and honesty he looks for in acting are artistic equivalents for the sincerity and equanimity he is searching for in real life. He wants a true friend who "is not passion's slave," and he does not want an actor to "out-Herod Herod" by expressing passion in an exaggerated way. He wants clowns "not to speak more than is set down" for them, and he wants Polonius not to be a "tedious old fool." For a man with Hamlet's ideals the world is out of joint with itself; only in art, which is made consciously, can he hope for perfection.

**13.** Hamlet's confrontation with the gravedigger, a man happy enough to sing at his work even while surrounded by death, teaches Hamlet that "the readiness is all"—that there is no escaping one's destiny—and that all paths lead to the grave. At the same time, the gravedigger reveals to Hamlet how time passes, altering everything in a natural way. The gravedigger began his work the day Hamlet's father defeated Fortinbras and Hamlet himself was born. The skull they handle is that of Yorick, the court jester, who was in his way a second father to Hamlet, warm and loving, and a jovial drinking companion and practical joker to the gravedigger. Now he is only a skull, and his bones are being shoveled aside to make room for the young Ophelia. Death, it seems, cannot be depended on to respect youth and innocence any more than it respects age, wisdom, or strength.

**14.** First, the speech is significant as an example of Hamlet's refined taste, since it comes from a play too learned and intelligently written to be popular. Next, the story it contains reflects on Hamlet's situation. Pyrrhus, who kills King Priam in revenge for the murder of his father, Achilles, is a model of the man of action, which Hamlet craves to be. The second section of the speech describes the grief of Priam's wife, Hecuba, after his death, and thus is both a criticism of Gertrude (who has not shown a similar degree of grief over her husband King Hamlet) and a warning to Hamlet of the emotions he may trigger if he kills her new husband.

The speech both urges Hamlet on to action and puts him off by showing him the difference between his own behavior and that of a mythological king. The First Player's real tears and his sincerity in delivering the speech torment Hamlet, because they remind him of his own conflicting impulses and of his inability to feel sufficient desire for revenge or sufficient grief over his father's death.

**15.**    Comedy is necessary in a tragic work to give respite to the tragic feelings we experience. It also heightens and intensifies the tragic emotion by its extreme contrast. Comedy and tragedy are entwined in *Hamlet*, because the tragic hero himself is both a partly comic character and a master of witty repartee even while under the strongest emotional pressure. Hamlet has the disturbing gift of laughing at his own grief as well as at the shortcomings of the world in general. His laughter strengthens the plot, by becoming one of the qualities of his mind that enable him to evade his mission and postpone his revenge. In his own mind Hamlet is a fool, trapped in tragedy by the fact that the rest of the world is made up of even bigger fools, who lack his ability to laugh at himself. Claudius does not see anything funny in his situation as a murderer and as an incestuous husband; but Hamlet, calling him "my mother" and "uncle-father" can joke about it. The only character with whom Hamlet is wholly serious is Gertrude; he even calls his father's ghost "old mole."

# Term Paper Ideas

## Characters

Choose one of the following groups and compare the characters to each other in terms of their role in the action of the play:

1. Laertes, Fortinbras, and Horatio
2. Claudius and his brother
3. Hamlet and Ophelia
4. Polonius and Horatio
5. Claudius and Hamlet

## Imagery

Take one of the following images that recur repeatedly in the text of *Hamlet* and locate as many of its appearances in the play as you can. Show how Shakespeare develops and enriches the image by constantly varying it till it has an overall meaning for the play:

1. Poison in the ear
2. A mirror (or "glass")
3. Disease and rotting things
4. The sun
5. Acting and hypocrisy
6. Madness

## Externals

The following subjects are discussed only in passing or by implication in the play. Drawing on all the information Shakespeare gives, create as full a picture as you can of one of them:

1. Denmark's diplomatic relations with Poland, Norway, and England

2. Actors and their position in society

3. The rights and status of women at court

4. The changing attitude of the Danish people toward the royal family

## Hamlet in Thought and Action

Take one of these decisive moments in Hamlet's story and analyze it in terms of Hamlet's own philosophic view, in terms of his goal of revenge, and in terms of today's moral standards. Discuss whether his action is justifiable and practical by each set of terms:

1. The confrontation with Ophelia (the Nunnery Scene)

2. His behavior during the Play Scene

3. The killing of Polonius

4. His treatment of his mother in the Closet Scene

5. His argument with Laertes at the graveyard

6. The killing of Rosencrantz and Guildenstern

## Hamlet and Our Times

Take one of the following topics central to *Hamlet*, and discuss it in terms of what the play has to say to modern readers. In what way does Hamlet's life tell you something about yours on these subjects:

1. Suicide

2. Love and marriage

3. Mother-son relations

4. Honest government

# Further Reading

## CRITICAL WORKS

Bevington, David, ed. *Hamlet: Twentieth Century Interpretations.* New York: Prentice-Hall, 1960. An excellent anthology of excerpts from most of the major modern commentators on the play.

Bradley, A. C. *Shakespearean Tragedy.* New York: Macmillan, 1955. The first description of the "melancholic" Hamlet.

Bullough, Geoffrey. *Narrative and Dramatic Sources of Shakespeare,* vol. 7. New York: Columbia University Press, 1973. Contains translations of the story of "Amleth" from both Saxo Grammaticus and François de Belleforest, plus many excerpts from Elizabethan works. Also gives possible sources for various parts of *Hamlet.*

Granville-Barker, Harley. *Prefaces to Shakespeare,* vol. 1. Princeton: Princeton University Press, 1946. A detailed analysis by an important stage director and theorist.

Grebanier, Bernard. *The Heart of Hamlet.* New York: T.Y. Crowell, 1960. A "healthy" interpretation of Hamlet.

Jones, Ernest. *Hamlet and Oedipus.* New York: Anchor Books, 1949. The influential Freudian analysis.

Levin, Harry. *The Question of Hamlet.* New York: Oxford University Press, 1959. An excellent analysis of the play's structure and modes of diction.

Nagler, Alois M. *Shakespeare's Stage.* New Haven: Yale University Press, 1981. The standard work on the physical space of the theaters in which Shakespeare performed.

Salgado, Gamini, ed. *Eyewitnesses to Shakespeare.* New York: Barnes & Noble, 1975. An anthology of excerpts from reviews and comments on performances of Shakespeare's plays in England from 1590–1890.

Schoenbaum, S. *Shakespeare: The Globe and the World.* New York: Oxford University Press, 1979. A lavishly illustrated summary of Shakespeare's life and times, particularly good on the historical background.

Shattuck, Charles H. *Shakespeare on the American Stage.* Washington, D.C.: Folger Shakespeare Library, 1978. History of Shakespearean acting in America up to the late nineteenth century, with detailed descriptions of about twenty Hamlets, including Edwin Booth.

Thomson, Peter. *Shakespeare's Theatre.* London: Routledge & Kegan Paul, 1983. An excellent work on the Globe Theatre, summarizing available information on audience, costumes, acting style, atmosphere, company management, etc.

Tillyard, E.M.W. *The Elizabethan World Picture.* New York: Random House, 1959. Essays on the politics, philosophy, and social structure of Shakespeare's time.

Wilson, J. Dover. *What Happens in Hamlet.* Cambridge: Cambridge University Press, 1935. A detailed summary, full of insight on many specific points.

## AUTHOR'S OTHER WORKS

Shakespeare wrote 37 plays (38 if you include *The Two Noble Kinsmen*) over a 20-year period, from about 1590 to 1610. It's difficult to determine the exact dates when many were written, but scholars have made the following intelligent guesses about his plays and poems:

**Plays**

| | |
|---|---|
| 1588–93 | *The Comedy of Errors* |
| 1588–94 | *Love's Labor's Lost* |
| 1590–91 | *2 Henry VI* |
| 1590–91 | *3 Henry VI* |
| 1591–92 | *1 Henry VI* |
| 1592–93 | *Richard III* |
| 1592–94 | *Titus Andronicus* |
| 1593–94 | *The Taming of the Shrew* |
| 1593–95 | *The Two Gentlemen of Verona* |

| 1594–96 | *Romeo and Juliet* |
| 1595 | *Richard II* |
| 1594–96 | *A Midsummer Night's Dream* |
| 1596–97 | *King John* |
| 1596–97 | *The Merchant of Venice* |
| 1597 | *1 Henry IV* |
| 1597–98 | *2 Henry IV* |
| 1598–1600 | *Much Ado About Nothing* |
| 1598–99 | *Henry V* |
| 1599 | *Julius Caesar* |
| 1599–1600 | *As You Like It* |
| 1599–1600 | *Twelfth Night* |
| 1600–01 | *Hamlet* |
| 1597–1601 | *The Merry Wives of Windsor* |
| 1601–02 | *Troilus and Cressida* |
| 1602–04 | *All's Well That Ends Well* |
| 1603–04 | *Othello* |
| 1604 | *Measure for Measure* |
| 1605–06 | *King Lear* |
| 1605–06 | *Macbeth* |
| 1606–07 | *Antony and Cleopatra* |
| 1605–08 | *Timon of Athens* |
| 1607–09 | *Coriolanus* |
| 1608–09 | *Pericles* |
| 1609–10 | *Cymbeline* |
| 1610–11 | *The Winter's Tale* |
| 1611–12 | *The Tempest* |
| 1612–13 | *Henry VIII* |

**Poems**

| 1592 | *Venus and Adonis* |
| 1593–94 | *The Rape of Lucrece* |
| 1593–1600 | *Sonnets* |
| 1600–01 | *The Phoenix and the Turtle* |

# The Critics

Probably more criticism has been written about *Hamlet* than about any other work of literature in the English language. The changing views of Hamlet as a character are summarized in the Characters section of this guide. The following quotes are a sampling of major views of the play over the past three centuries. They are intended to open the discussion for you, not end it.

## EIGHTEENTH CENTURY

. . . we must allow to the tragedy of *Hamlet* the praise of variety. The incidents are so numerous, that the argument [summary] of the play would make a long tale. . . . The action is indeed for the most part in continual progression, but there are some scenes which neither forward nor retard it. Of the feigned madness of Hamlet there appears no adequate cause, for he does nothing which he might not have done with the reputation of sanity. He plays the madman most, when he treats Ophelia with so much rudeness, which seems to be useless and wanton cruelty.

*Samuel Johnson, from the notes to his Edition of Shakespeare's Dramatic Works, 1765*

Tender and nobly descended, this royal flower [Hamlet] grew up under the direct influences of majesty; the idea of the right and of princely dignity, the feeling for the good and the graceful, with the consciousness of his high birth, were unfolded in him together. He was a prince, a born prince. Pleasing in figure, polished by nature, courteous from the heart, he was to be the model of youth and the delight of the world. . . . A beautiful, pure, noble and most moral nature, without the strength of nerve which makes a hero, sinks beneath a burden which it can neither bear nor throw off. . . .

*Johann Wolfgang von Goethe, from* Wilhelm Meister, *Book V, 1795*

## NINETEENTH CENTURY

One of Shakespeare's modes of creating characters is to conceive any one intellectual or moral faculty in morbid excess, and then to place himself, Shakespeare, thus mutilated or diseased, under given circumstances. In Hamlet he seems to have wished to exemplify the moral necessity of a due balance—between our attention to the objects of our sense and our meditation on the working of our minds—an equilibrium between the real and the imaginary worlds. In Hamlet this balance is disturbed; his thoughts and the images of his fancy are far more vivid than his actual perceptions. . . . Hence we see a great, an almost enormous, intellectual activity, and a proportionate aversion to real action consequent upon it. . . . This character Shakespeare places in circumstances under which he is obliged to act on the spur of the moment: Hamlet is brave and careless of death; but he vacillates from sensibility, and procrastinates from thought, and loses the power of action in the energy of resolve. . . . He mistakes the seeing of his chains for the breaking of them, delays action till action is of no use, and dies the victim of mere circumstance and accident.

*Samuel Taylor Coleridge, from* Notes and Lectures on Shakespeare, *1808*

Hamlet is single in its kind: A tragedy of thought inspired by continual and never-satisfied meditation on human destiny and the dark perplexity of the events of this world, calculated to call forth the very same meditation in the minds of the spectators. . . . Respecting Hamlet's character, I cannot pronounce altogether so favorable a judgment as Goethe's. . . . The weakness of his volition is evident: He does himself only justice when he says there is no greater dissimilarity than between himself and Hercules. He is not solely impelled by necessity to artifice and dissimulation; he has a natural inclination to go crooked ways; he is a hypocrite towards himself; his far-fetched scruples are

often mere pretexts to cover his lack of resolution
. . . he is too much overwhelmed with his own
sorrow to have any compassion to spare for others. . . . On the other hand we evidently perceive
in him a malicious joy when he has succeeded in
getting rid of his enemies more through necessity
and accident, which are alone able to impel him to
quick and decisive measures, than from the merit
of his courage. . . . Hamlet has no firm belief in
himself or anything else. . . . The destiny of
humanity is here exhibited as a gigantic Sphinx,
which threatens to precipitate into the abyss of
skepticism whoever is unable to solve her dreadful
enigma.

*August Wilhelm Schlegel, from*
Lectures on Art and Dramatic
Literature, *1809*

Hamlet is a name: His speeches and sayings but
the idle coinage of the poet's brain. What, then are
they not real? They are as real as our own
thoughts. Their reality is in the reader's mind. It is
*we* who are Hamlet. . . . We have been so used to
this tragedy, that we hardly know how to criticize
it, any more than we should know how to describe
our own faces. . . . It is the one of Shakespeare's
plays that we think of oftenest, because it abounds
most in striking reflections on human life, and
because the distresses of Hamlet are transferred by
the turn of his mind, to the general account of
humanity. Whatever happens to him we apply to
ourselves, because he applies it to himself as a
means of general reasoning. . . . [He] is not a character marked by strength of will, or even of passion, but by refinement of thought and sentiment.
. . . He is the prince of philosophical speculators,
and because he cannot have his revenge perfect,
according to the most refined idea his wish can
form, he misses it altogether. . . . His ruling passion is to think, not to act; and any vague pretense
that flatters this propensity instantly diverts him
from his previous purposes. . . . The character of

Hamlet is made up of undulating lines; it has the
yielding flexibility of 'a wave o' th' sea.'

> *William Hazlitt, from* Characters of
> Shakespeare's Plays, *1812*

[Hamlet] is not master of his acts; occasion dictates
them; he cannot plan a murder, but must impro-
vise it. A too-lively imagination exhausts energy
by the accumulation of images, and by the fury of
intentness which absorbs it. You recognize in him
a poet's soul, made not to act but to dream, which
is lost in contemplating the phantoms of its own
creation, which sees the imaginary world too clearly to play a part in the real world; an artist whom
evil chance has made a prince, whom worse
chance has made an avenger of crime, and who,
destined by nature for genius, is condemned by
fortune to madness and unhappiness.

> *Hippolyte-Adolphe Taine, from* History
> of English Literature, *1866*

Much discussion has turned on the question of
Hamlet's madness, whether it be real or assumed.
It is not possible to settle this question. . . . Shakespeare meant Hamlet to be in a state of *intense cere-
bral excitement*, seeming like madness. His sorrow-
ing nature has suddenly been ploughed to its
depths by a horror so great as to make him recoil
every moment from a belief in its reality. The
shock, if it has not destroyed his sanity, has certainly *unsettled* him.

> *George Henry Lewes, from* On Actors
> and the Art of Acting, *1875*

[Hamlet] is a man in whom the common personal
passions are so superseded by wider and rarer
interests, and so discouraged by a degree of critical
self-consciousness which makes the practical effi-
ciency of the instinctive man on the lower plane
impossible to him, that he finds the duties dictated
by conventional revenge and ambition as disagree-
able a burden as commerce is to a poet. Even his
instinctive sexual impulses offend his intellect; so

that when he meets the woman who excites them he invites her to join him in a bitter and scornful criticism of their joint absurdity . . . all of which is so completely beyond the poor girl that she naturally thinks him mad. And, indeed, there is a sense in which Hamlet is insane; for he trips over the mistake which lies on the threshold of intellectual self-consciousness: That of bringing life to utilitarian or Hedonistic tests, thus treating it as a means instead of an end.

> *George Bernard Shaw, from his review of Johnston Forbes-Robertson's production of the play, in* Our Theatres in the Nineties, *Vol. 3, 1897*

# TWENTIETH CENTURY

One would judge that by temperament [Hamlet] was inclined to nervous instability, to rapid and perhaps extreme changes of feeling or mood. . . . This temperament the Elizabethans would have called melancholic. . . . Next, we cannot be mistaken in attributing to [him] an exquisite sensibility to which we may give the name "moral." . . . To the very end, his soul, however sick and tortured it may be, answers instantaneously when good and evil are presented to it, loving the one and hating the other. . . . Now, in Hamlet's moral sensibility there undoubtedly lay a danger. Any great shock that life might inflict on it would be felt with extreme intensity. Such a shock might even produce tragic results. . . .

> *A. C. Bradley, from* Shakespearean Tragedy, *Lecture 3, 1904*

So far from being Shakespeare's masterpiece, the play is most certainly an artistic failure. In several ways [it] is puzzling and disquieting as is none of the others. . . . Probably more people have thought *Hamlet* a work of art because they found it interesting, than have found it interesting because it is a work of art. It is the "Mona Lisa" of literature. . . . The only way of expressing emotion in the form of art is by finding an "objective correlative"; in other words, a set of objects, a situation, a chain of events which shall be the formula of that particular emotion . . . and this is precisely what is deficient in *Hamlet*. Hamlet (the man) is dominated by an emotion which is inexpressible, because it is in *excess* of the facts as they appear. . . . Hamlet is up against the difficulty that his disgust is occasioned by his mother, but his mother is not an adequate equivalent for it; his disgust envelops and exceeds her. It is thus a feeling which he cannot understand; he cannot objectify it, and it therefore remains to poison life and obstruct action. None of the possible actions can satisfy it; and nothing that Shakespeare can do with the plot can express Hamlet for him. . . . We must simply admit that here Shakespeare tackled a problem that proved too much for him. Why he attempted it at all is an insoluble puzzle; under compulsion of what experience he attempted to express the inexpressibly horrible, we cannot ever know.

> T. S. Eliot, from "Hamlet and His Problems," in Selected Essays, 1920

Whenever a person cannot bring himself to do something that every conscious consideration tells him he should do—and which he may have the strongest conscious desire to do—it is always because there is some hidden reason why a part of him doesn't want to do it; this reason he will not own to himself and is only dimly, if at all, aware of. That is exactly the case with Hamlet. . . . The more intense and the more obscure is a case of deep mental conflict, the more certainly will it be found on adequate analysis to center about a sexual problem. . . . [Hamlet's] long "repressed" desire to take his father's place in his mother's affection is stimulated to unconscious activity by the sight of someone usurping this place exactly as he himself had once longed to do. More, this someone was a member of the same family, so that the actual usurpation further resembled the imaginary one in being incestuous. Without his being in the least aware of it, the ancient desires are ringing in his mind, are once more struggling to find conscious expression, and need such an expenditure of energy again to "repress" them that he is reduced to the deplorable mental state he himself so vividly depicts.

*Ernest Jones, from* Hamlet and
Oedipus, *1949*

Yet his soul's adventure, which seemed but to lead him to defeat, was heroic too. For if men shirk such perils, how are these high matters to be brought home to spiritual freedom? Nor will mere intellectual venturing suffice, if lively faith, in its health and strength, is to be found and enjoyed again. Hamlet, being called upon, flings his whole being—mind and affections both, the best and the worst of him, weakness no less than strength—into the trial. And he widens the issue till he sees eternal life and death, his own and his enemy's, at stake. He will reconcile himself, as he is and in all he is, with these now unveiled verities of this world and the next, if that may be. In which Promethean struggle towards the light he is beaten—as who has not been?—with havoc wrought, not in him only, but by him, even to his own despite. It is none the less a heroic struggle.

Here, for me, is the master-clue to Hamlet's "mystery." The "sane" world around him has naturally no sense of it, nor the too sane spectator of the play. He does not pluck out the heart of it himself. Neither are we meant to. For his trouble is rooted in the fact that it is a mystery.

*Harley Granville-Barker, in* Prefaces to
Shakespeare, *Vol. I, 1946*

# NOTES